Crabdance

crabdance

beverley simons

published with assistance from the Canada Council

Talonbooks
201 1019 East Cordova
Vancouver
British Columbia V6A 1M8
Canada

This book was designed by Gordon Fidler and printed by Hemlock Printers for Talonbooks.

Fifth printing: December 1976

Talonplays are edited by Peter Hay.

Cover drawing by Claude Breeze.

First published by In Press, Vancouver, B.C.

Canadian Shared Cataloguing in Publication Data

Simons, Beverley, 1938-
Crabdance

ISBN 0-88922-016-6 pa.

I. Title.
PS8587 C812'.5'4
PR9199.3

"In the springtime, giant Alaska crabs lock claws and drag each other over the ocean floor. The female moults. Copulation follows. The male remains to guard the female until she's grown a new shell."

introduction

In the foreword to an earlier edition of this book I began by remarking, "this play has a peculiar stage history – most of it has taken place offstage." That edition was in conjunction with the Canadian premiere of *Crabdance* at the Vancouver Playhouse in January, 1972. Since then that stage history has become, if anything, more peculiar. Apart from a few studio productions, neither our regional nor the two so-called national theatres in Ottawa and Stratford have shown the slightest inclination to present *Crabdance*. In fact, with this current edition we have reached the somewhat unusual situation that there have been more printings of the book than professional stage productions of the play.

This would be readily explicable if *Crabdance* were considered a mediocre or indifferent work of topical interest. After all, theatre is, by its very nature, a transitory art; the vast majority of new plays presented in any global season die with it. For a precious few, however, five years is a kind of immortality. But *Crabdance* is acknowledged by a number of critics and theatre professionals as certainly one of the finest, if not the finest dramatic work yet written in Canada. It is being taught at an increasing number of universities, CBC radio has made a full-length recording of it and as this edition goes into print, the Alberta government's TV station, ACCESS, is making a videotape version of the Citadel Theatre's production of *Crabdance*, directed by Malcolm Black, which soon will be made available to schools. If Beverley Simons had written a novel with the same power that the play carries, her name would be as well known in Canada as that of Margaret Atwood or anyone else from this generation.

A drama, however, whatever its literary qualities, can only reach a wide audience through a number of productions. The playwright cannot speak directly to the reader, only through interpreters: producers, directors, actors – in short, the theatrical profession. And the profession, on the whole, has yet to discover those fairly obvious qualities that make *Crabdance* an outstanding piece of theatre.

Since it was first produced and published, the play has become quite well-known to producers and artistic directors who make decisions about what the Canadian theatre public might be allowed to see. Apart from an honest few who have stated that they dislike or at least lack empathy with *Crabdance*, the majority assert that the play is "difficult," a catch-all excuse that seems to apply exclusively to Canadian drama. What – in the name of Shakespeare, G.B.S. or Brecht – is so difficult about *Crabdance*?

There are many works, especially among the classics and historical dramas, which are prohibitively expensive because of the size of the cast, sets and costumes. This play has four major characters and one set. Most Canadian companies, despite the cost, manage to produce one or two large-canvas plays a season, usually by British or American authors. To my knowledge, Shakespeare has not written a play for four characters.

Crabdance does require, of course, a director who is alive to its many levels of emotion and meaning – what good play does not? Also needed are some first-rate actors and especially an actress who can play Sadie Golden – to quote the author – "with her legs uncrossed." But the Canadian theatre has produced a number of fine actors and three or four magnificent actresses. It, however, has only one Beverley Simons. Now, if somebody were to claim that it is difficult to make Shakespeare or Ben Jonson enjoyable to a modern Canadian audience, I might nod sympathetically and hope to dissuade the person from trying. But in terms of money, resources, talent or intelligibility *Crabdance* can be produced very easily. All it takes is the will and commitment to go ahead. But such commitment is in short supply. Hence, the mythology that it is a difficult play.

Another myth was discussed in a special issue of the *Canadian Theatre Review* (*CTR 9*, Winter, 1976) devoted to the work of Beverley Simons, the first time that publication so honoured a playwright. Although her reputation is mainly based on *Crabdance*, this gives a false impression that it is the only or even her major work. Simons has created in the last decade three original feature film scenarios, four or five evenings of theatre, and several stories and shorter works. Her last completed drama, *Leela Means to Play*, (published in *CTR*) is a massive work, full of innovation and likely to confound theatre professionals and critics for years to come. The point is that Simons has left *Crabdance* long behind in her art, while many people in our theatre and universities still need to catch up with it.

Dr. Bertram Joseph, the well known Shakespeare scholar and critic wrote after *Crabdance*'s premiere in Seattle:

> I am not afraid to use the word "great" of
> this play. I am more certain it is great than I
> am that Beckett's *Waiting For Godot* is great.
> *Crabdance* is great in its vision of life . . .

What, briefly, is that vision?

The commonplaces of everyday existence and emotions are transmuted in this tragicomedy into an elaborate and progressive ritual. The games Sadie plays with her salesmen reflect the desire for those normal ties a woman has with her son, her husband and her lover. These relationships in the play may be largely symbolic, but the emotional need for them, on the part of both the salesmen and of their client, is totally real.

The characters move in the stylized, bitter-sweet world of the *commedia dell'arte*: their exaggerated antics become truer with each added absurdity. The final vision of the play, as seen through Sadie's terrifying self-knowledge, is tragic. Her dance progresses from Mowchuk's initiation, through the convention-bound Dickens to the hollow fascination of Highrise, and we see it turn into a *danse macabre*. When she dies her appointed death, the last laugh is on her, because Sadie knows – like the actress who plays her – that she will perform the ritual once more the next day. But we can no longer laugh either at or with her.

Despite the difficulties some people have, because *Crabdance* does not seem to be set in rural Ontario and makes no mention of West Coast Indians, it is still a fundamentally Canadian play. As in her earlier stage works, "The Elephant and the Jewish Question," and in her volume of short plays, *Preparing*, Beverley Simons draws passion and strength from her ethnic as well as Prairie background. Much of the tension and some of the humour in *Crabdance* comes from the natural antagonism between the Anglo-Saxon Dickens and the Ukrainian Mowchuk. Sadie represents other minorities through her Jewishness and simply by being a woman. The most broadly satirical character is Highrise, whom Westerners will identify as the Eastern con-man trying to acquire prestige through imaginary and imitative exploits south of the border.

By an odd co-incidence, and perhaps luckily for casting the play, all these characters have easily identifiable counterparts in the present-day Canadian theatre.

Perhaps the greatest puzzle to playwrights, and maybe to audiences, is how artistic directors acquire the intuitions of knowing so exactly what the Canadian public wants. What makes them so certain about what they don't want?

After a trip to Toronto, Beverley Simons came back home with a true story, which I offer to all directors in this country. She had the usual experiences in that great cultural Mecca to which most artists from the West Coast or any other region are treated. She felt the fatigue of having to explain who she was and what she had been doing over the past ten years or so. She heard respected directors explain to her that the average audience in Canada was not "ready" yet for *Crabdance*. After a few days of this, thoroughly worn-out, frustrated and disenchanted, she and her husband took a cab one evening. A conversation, mainly about politics, with this regular cabbie, led to mutual introductions. After all, it was the first intelligent discussion the Simons' had had in Toronto.

"You wouldn't be the Beverley Simons who wrote that play . . . *Crabdance*?" asked the cabdriver, only somewhat less amazed than the author herself. He had a friend, it turned out, working the the logging camps of northern British Columbia, who really enjoys reading playscripts, which he then sends on to his buddy in Toronto. "And the one person I remember most strongly is that Sadie Golden . . ."

Peter Hay
Fort Langley, B.C.
December, 1976

Crabdance was first performed at A Contemporary Theatre in Seattle, Washington, U.S.A., on September 16, 1969, with the following cast:

Sadie	Marjorie Nelson
Mowchuk	Robert Casper
Dickens	Alan Scarfe
Highrise	Gordon Gould

Directed by Malcolm Black

Crabdance was also performed at the Playhouse Theatre Centre in Vancouver, British Columbia, on January 14, 1972, with the following cast:

Sadie	Jennifer Phipps
Mowchuk	Hutchinson Shandro
Dickens	Sandy Webster
Highrise	Neil Dainard

Directed by Frances Hyland
Designed by Cam Porteous

act one

A living room, dining room area, entrance hall and entrance to a kitchen. Free-standing stairs end abruptly in space above the set. The upper portion of the stairs leading to the voice may be obscured at first by a wall and exposed only at the three o'clock glare. The stage front represents a plate glass window.

The set should be suggestive rather than detailed, and though the furniture is real, the effect should be curiously disturbing. The furniture is shrouded in cowl-like sheets. Each piece has a character of its own, related to its function and to the person who will belong to it.

Scattered on the sheet which covers the dining room table are mounds of writing paper, envelopes, letters, lists, newspaper clippings and a pair of scissors. A wall phone hangs between the dining room area and the kitchen. Pinned beside the phone is an exaggeratedly long sheet of foolscap filled with names and several large advertisements.

A large, blue china cat with an enormous belly filled with SADIE's savings stands in a conspicuous position on the floor, and nearby, there is a box filled with advertisements.

SADIE is in her fifties, now thin, sagging, highly nervous. Smiles appear and disappear involuntarily on her face. She makes little noises without being aware of them. The word "hunh." when it appears in the text, merely indicates a place for the use of her sounds. She emanates a strange combination of vulnerability and threat, naivete and cunning.

As the play opens, SADIE is in the midst of hurried preparations.

SADIE:

Listen, you can't kid me about making woman out of man's ribs. You wouldn't change your mind about how to do things right off the bat. I mean, God doesn't make mistakes. First shot, bango, right on target. So why ribs first and then wombs? Man springs from woman, it's in your book.

Come on, you can tell me. Nobody's listening. It's a cover-up, right? You don't want us to know you had a bit of pleasure with the first woman. You shouldn't be ashamed. Immaculate Conception! Pheh! That must have been some fight before you got her down. *With appreciation.* Or maybe you haven't told because you don't want the other women, me, to take a real look at what we're left with . . . Mortal lovers.

She spits, then sings the following song, using a simple three-pitch melody that will be used throughout the play.

How she loved her darling man.
She wound her arms around him.
But when she woke,
Her man was gone.
A baby had replaced him.

The last line is spoken. After a pause, she resumes her work.

They'll be here soon. We better hurry. What'll they think if we're not ready for them? They'll think we're slops, that's what. Hunh. They won't come back. They'll come back.

Hunh, hunh. Wouldn't Golden be jealous if he knew about this afternoon! It's not my fault I attract friends. It's a gift from God. You could as soon cut off my arms, I told him. I wonder if he can hear me.

SADIE looks to her imagined location of heaven, up the staircase to the second floor and beyond. She shouts to "The Old Man," Golden.

Can you hear me? Like Jehovah, he hears me. The two of them up there playing stupid. Wouldn't the neighbours be surprised if he answered! Either of them.

A bell or the buzzer of a stove in the kitchen is heard.

My tarts.

She dashes into the kitchen. The sound of pans being removed from the oven is heard. She re-enters the living room.

Pumpkin for Mr. Dickens, strawberry for Mr. Wilkins, blood pudding for Mr. Highrise, sugar cookies, date cookies, chocolate cookies, meat balls, rice balls, chicken soup, duck soup, oh dear, oh dear, oh dear . . .

It's starting. My breasts. I can feel them. Muscles, tick tick.

They're my two white sacs, no, collapsed globes, maps of blue veins and white stretch lines, meaning nothing until they . . . yes, starting, swell and fill, full . . . Then whole worlds can be read on them. My nipples corks of fire. Burn! I want to hurt. The pain pleasures me. MILK!

SADIE falls over the blue cat. The sound of the cash inside it is heard.

Under my feet again! Why are you always under my feet? Why don't you stay in your place where you're put where I put you?

Are you hurt? Puss puss? Nothing lost?

SADIE rocks the cat and hums comfortingly. Sounds from the cat and SADIE's sound mix with the muted rumble of an approaching trolley.

Listen! The one o'clock trolley. Here it comes. Sparks on the wire like . . . like fireworks. He's dropped a cable! The conductor will get out and knock on our door. "May I have a glass of water?" Like last year. The blonde one. Remember? *Suddenly concerned.* We won't have room for him this time. *She looks out again.* No. *Sadly.* Gone. *She stops shaking the jar.* You are a liar, old woman. You're dry. You sag. Why don't you throw them away, Sadie, with the old vacuum cleaner bags?

The phone rings. SADIE answers it.

Hello? Sadie Golden speaking. I'm always in. *Dryly.* Of course I remember who you are, Mr. . . . *She runs her fingers down the list pinned on the wall.* Schwartz. This afternoon? *She touches her hair self-consciously.* I'll have to rush to straighten up, but . . . How is three o'clock? Oh, did I mention it in my letter? I'll expect you then. And Mr. Schwartz, we'll use the silver tea service this time.

She hangs up the phone.

Schwartz . . . coming.

In a businesslike way she puts a check mark beside Schwartz's name, then fingers a stack of invitations on the dining room table.

Too late for these.

She drops them in a wastebasket. Reconsidering, she pulls one out again.

One more. Mister . . . Underhill. Our party wouldn't be complete without him. Out of the garbage. He'd appreciate that. *She writes quickly.* Special delivery. R.S.V.P. *She licks the envelope.*

The phone rings again.

Hello? Yes. Three o'clock. It can't be later. I look forward to seeing you, Mr. Goodman.

She hangs up. She puts another check on her list.

Whooo! I'm falling off my feet, but I can't disappoint them. You're too soft, Sadie Golden, that's your trouble. You've never learned to say no, have you? Look at your hands. Not very pretty. And the veins. Wouldn't it be embarrassing if they popped and spattered all over the teacups? I'll wear gloves. I don't want them to know how hard I've worked for them. *She reconsiders.* One glove? Well, you can't pour tea with gloves on. What if . . . they don't come? None of them.

A moment of dull panic, then SADIE rushes to her source of reassurance, the windows that open out on an artery of the city. She stares out, trying to suck the life she sees into her body. Next she must get that body busy. She sprays and polishes as she talks.

Plate glass, a real invention! We're lucky to be living here, you and I, Puss. Right in the centre of things. The whole world passes in front of us. No surprises left. Not for you and me. We've been here too long. We can't be lonely even if we want to.

SADIE starts to sing.

Bye baby bunting,
Mama's goin' a hunting,
The world is round
And though you run
You'll end up here with the setting sun,
My baby . . .

Her song is interrupted.

Hey, there goes Old Man Gerd. Pretends he can't see us. I know where the sun is. The glare's not till three o'clock. *She makes an appropriate thumb gesture.* Up yours, Gerd!

MOWCHUK enters.

He looked! He saw us, Puss! He saw us!

SADIE's movement brings into her vision the non-descript stranger standing in the living-room doorway. It is MOWCHUK, the rabbit, the son-to-be. In his late thirties, small boned, he overarticulates to cover a trace of accent. He carries a briefcase filled with books.

I didn't hear you come in.

MOWCHUK:
I . . . I knocked. The door . . . it opened by itself. It must have been off the catch . . . the latch.

SADIE approaches MOWCHUK even as he speaks and circles him, examining him, touching him with short, hesitant hand movements, first the material of his jacket, his fingers, perhaps even his face; sniffing even. as though she were blind and could only read him through fingers and nostrils; yet her eyes feel MOW-CHUK too, but in pieces, disembodying him.

SADIE: *sniffing his jacket*
Jacket . . . not bad.

MOWCHUK: *during this process*
Shall I go away? I can come back later, another time. *Hopefully.* Tomorrow?

SADIE:
Hands . . .

MOWCHUCK: *as he pulls his briefcase back*
My briefcase!

SADIE:
. . . small. Everything hunh there, as far as meets the eye.

MOWCHUK instinctively covers his crotch.

What do you think, Puss. Hunh? Will he do? Not exactly what we had in mind for our first born . . . But a woman can't choose.

MOWCHUK:
I . . . I . . .

SADIE: *still to the cat*
He stutters! A handicap at a party.

She turns on him suddenly.

You're early! I'm not angry. Don't be frightened. I'm flattered. You couldn't wait to get here. *To Puss.* He couldn't wait, Puss. To reach us. Impatient. Just like a man. We can use a man's back. You can help me get things in order. A party's a delicate thing, Mr. . .

MOWCHUK: *searches his mind desperately*
Mmmmmmm . . . Mmmmmmm . . .

SADIE:
Yes?

MOWCHUK:
Mmmmaaa . : .

SADIE: *encouraging*
That's it.

MOWCHUK:
Ma . . . Ma . . .

SADIE:
Good boy! You got it!

MOWCHUK:
Mmmmmowchuk. Leonard Mowchuk. Leonard Mowchuk.

SADIE:
How do you do, Mr. Mowchuk? Sadie Golden.

Élegantly she holds out her hand to him. As he deliberates whether or not to touch it, she changes the gesture into a wave, indicating chairs.

Won't you sit down?

Hypnotized. MOWCHUK goes goward the large sheeted chair

I said, sit down.

MOWCHUK starts to obey.

Not there. Over here. *She leads him.*

He's perfect for the training chair, don't you agree, Puss? At least until we get to know him better. People don't understand these things nowadays, Mr. Mowchuk. Parties have to be shaped.

MOWCHUK has started to sit in the indicated chair.

Wait!

He stands up again. Ceremoniously, reverently, SADIE removes the sheet revealing a child's potty.

Guest number one.

She places her hands on MOWCHUK's shoulder, gently pressing him down. MOWCHUK opens his mouth as if to speak. SADIE gestures for silence.

Shhh. I want to remember.

MOWCHUK poses as though awaiting a photographer's flash. He forces a sick smile. Then SADIE poses beside him. Proud mother and son. Tintype style.

MOWCHUK: *blurting it out*
I'm not a guest.

SADIE: *just as suddenly hard*
Then you're a thief.

MOWCHUK:
No! At least, I don't think so. If anything I'm plagued by integrity.

SADIE:
You walked into my house.

MOWCHUK:
The door, I told you. It was like someone was on the other side pulling.

SADIE:
Are you suggesting . . .

MOWCHUK:
Nothing. I'm not anything.

SADIE:
I don't have to drag people in off the street. The phone, it doesn't stop. Or the doorbell. Day and night. Telegrams. Cables. It's "Help me! Should I do this, Sadie? Or should I do that? " Nobody stops to worry Sadie Golden maybe she's tired. My bones are glass. They've sucked the marrow out of them. I'm not complaining. There are some people . . . there are power centres, you know? You see them. Up on a hill or under a lake. Where all the wires and batteries and cables come together, they pulse . . .

For a moment, her strength is revealed. Suddenly, she is businesslike and hard again. To MOWCHUK.

You didn't wipe your feet.

MOWCHUK: *looking guiltily down at his shoes*
Shall I go back?

SADIE:
A thief would have wiped his feet so as not to leave tracks. The truth, Mr. Muffett . . .

MOWCHUK: *standing formlly, reciting his name*
Mowchuk. Leonard Mowchuk.

SADIE:

Can't be avoided. You're a guest. I expect you to behave like one. *In a complete change of tone.* Will you have tea? We should wait for the others, but one cup won't hurt.

Without waiting for a reply. SADIE exits to the kitchen for some tea.

MOWCHUK: *uncertain, to himself*

You could call it a visit, I suppose.

SADIE: *calling from the kitchen*

Don't be fooled by appearances, Mr. Mowchuk.

MOWCHUK: *to himself*

They didn't prepare me for anything like this. It's not fair.

SADIE:

The room looks like a funeral parlour to you. *The exaggerated sound of water being poured into a tea kettle is heard.* You didn't have to say it. I could read your face.

MOWCHUK: *still to himself*

Not at any of the lectures. Or in the pamphlets.

The high piercing whistle of the water boiling in the tea kettle is heard. MOWCHUK jumps.

A book . . . I must . . . hold . . . *He opens his case, gropes for and takes out a large tome.* Heavy . . . weight . . . Thank God! No! Control reflexes, Mowchuk. Reason. Data. *He fumbles in his inner jacket pocket and pulls out a measuring tape.* That's it. Facts.

With desperate concentration MOWCHUK measures the book. He kneels on the floor with the book on his chair seat.

Fourteen inches in length, twelve inches in width, four inches thickness, five thousand years content . . . No. Non sequitur. An immeasurable there.

SADIE has been beside him with tea things for part of his data speech.

SADIE:

Are you leaving? You can if you want to.

She sweeps the sheet from the coffee table and sets down the tray.

MOWCHUK is embarrassed at being caught. Trying to keep his back to SADIE, he hurriedly puts the book and the tape back into his briefcase.

If you're bored . . .

MOWCHUK:

No! Why should I be?

SADIE gives one end of the sheet to MOWCHUK.

SADIE:

You won't hurt my feelings . . .

MOWCHUK:

On the contrary, I . . .

They fold the sheet together.

SADIE:

There's no obligations. That's the first rule here. You walked into my house because you wanted to. Or so I gather. Now you're welcome to stay. Or go. Whichever you chose. *She starts to pour tea.*

MOWCHUK:
As a gentleman, Madam, I . . . I hardly . . .

SADIE:
You can't throw it at me later I didn't give you a chance. Sadie Golden hangs onto no one. But . . . if you do stay . . .

MOWCHUK:
Yes?

SADIE:
It gets harder and harder to leave.

MOWCHUK:
Why?

The phone rings.

SADIE:
See what I mean? It never stops. Not that I'm complaining.

She picks up the phone.

Hello? Yes, Reverend Cavil. *Running her pencil down her list.* You can't make it? *She puts an "X" beside his name.* Why should I be offended? *Stretching the phone cord, she moves toward the kitchen.* You come to see me whenever you like. It's not for me to choose. I'm surprised you want to talk to a silly old woman at all. Of course, I might not be at home when you do decide to come, but I'm sure you have so many others to visit you'll hardly notice. Yes. A little something, yes, Mr. Golden left me that. Thank you for your condolences. Your concern is touching. Tomorrow? I won't be here. No. Not the rest of the week either. I'm getting old, Reverend. It's as hard for me to hold back a decision as it is to hold my water.

MOWCHUK coughs.

Did I tell you that Rabbi Grubber will be here? Now why should you change your plans for me?

Although he is listening, MOWCHUK can't resist the impulse to peek under the sheets.

I wouldn't dream of interfering in a family crisis. *A pause.* You insist.

MOWCHUK is horrified at what he sees under one of the sheets – a coffin, unseen by the audience.

At three o'clock then.

SADIE re-enters to change the "X" to a check mark on the list, just in time to see MOWCHUK drop the corner of the crucial sheet.

Ah ah ah. Don't rush it, Mowchuk. You'll see everything in good time.

SADIE puts her hand affectionately on a covered piece of furniture.

They're in cocoons, waiting to be let out. You released your chair, Mr. Mowchuk. You've got to accept responsibility for it now. It's not complete unless Leonard Muffett . . .

MOWCHUK:
Mowchuk.

SADIE:
. . . is sitting on it. One by one my friends will break all the shells. This room will be as gay as a garden. Right, Puss? But I haven't introduced you . . .

SADIE notices MOWCHUK is staring at her.

Your face, it's . . . *She laughs, a surprisingly full throaty laugh.* You must have thought I was . . . talking to . . . I've been impolite.

She picks up the blue cat and carries it to MOWCHUK.

Puss, I'd like you to meet Mr. Mowchuk. Leonard Mowchuk. Leonard Mowchuk, Puss.

MOWCHUK: *weakly*
How do you do?

SADIE:
Go ahead. Pat her. Only if you want to. No? Maybe later. *To the cat.* You're better than flesh and blood, aren't you, Puss? You don't pull up threads from my furniture or shed hair on the cushions. No yowling at the door at night to go out. And you stay where you're put. Most of the time, that is. *To MOWCHUK.* Why aren't you drinking your tea?

MOWCHUK automatically takes a sip.

I had a real one once, a tabby, brown and white stripes.

Suddenly MOWCHUK notices a bouquet of flowers on the table. Inexplicably, it frightens him.

MOWCHUK: *involuntarily*
They're wax.

SADIE:
I was a slave to the seasons. The smell and the screams, You wouldn't believe it! He was killed by . . . *She looks out the window; rushes to it.* That dachshund! Shoo! Scat! He's at my spruce again. Sicked on by the neigh-

bour. I'm sure of it. She's jealous of that spruce. It's got the largest cones in the neighbourhood. Did you notice them when you came up the walk? Both sexes on the same bush. The big ones at the top are female.

SADIE is standing with her back to the window. Her body seems to grow and block out the light.

I'd had his claws pulled. Just the front ones. Because of the furniture. It was a perfectly painless operation. Or so the doctor said. Sugar?

MOWCHUK shakes his head no.

He also said he'd still be able to climb trees. I don't think he liked cats, that doctor. It was a terrible sight. Him scrambling up the tree trunk, and then sliding down again, up and down, up . . . while that . . . "animal" waited for him at the bottom, sniffing. It lacked dignity. At least it could have been a German Shepherd or a . . . a Black Labrador. There'd have been some splendour then. You really ought to, you know?

MOWCHUK:
Ought to . . . what?

SADIE:
Have sugar. Gives you energy. You remind me of my son. Did I tell you that? Same complexion. Same bone structure, here . . . *She touches MOWCHUK on the chin.* . . . here. *She touches him on the forehead around the temples.* One or two spoons?

MOWCHUK: *hypnotized*
Two.

SADIE:
Three?

MOWCHUK:
Three.

SADIE: *her hand still on his face*
When the time came, when they came of age, my son and my daughter, I said to them, "Go. Get out." For their good. That is, when they were ready for independence. *She puts three sugars in MOWCHUK's cup and stirs.* Tell me about you. You have something to say, haven't you? There was a reason that made you walk into my house.

MOWCHUK: *not believing that his time may have come*
Y . . . y . . . yes. Yes! Yes!

SADIE pings one of her teacups with a spoon.

I . . .

SADIE motions for silence until the sound ends.

SADIE:
That's its song. Leonard Mowchuk. What's yours?

MOWCHUK:
I'm a . . . I'm a . . .

SADIE is silent.

I'masalesman!

No reaction from SADIE. MOWCHUK standing, a prolonged call.

A saaaaaaalesmaaaaaaan!

SADIE:
Aren't we all?

MOWCHUK:
Not that way!

SADIE: *infinitely patient*
In what way, then?

MOWCHUK:
B . . . b . . . b . . . Books! I sell books! There. I've said it. I . . . I represent . . . *He looks at her imploringly. She says nothing.* I represent . . . How do you do Mrs. Golden, my name is Leonard Mowchuk and I represent THEUNIVERSALBOOKSOFKNOWLEDGE.

SADIE:
Whoo! Big name. A lot to represent.

MOWCHUK:
I . . . may not . . . ideally, that is, but . . . I don't matter, it's . . . it's what's in there, Mrs. Golden. *Tapping his briefcase.* Be . . . be . . . be . . . between these covers, in . . . in this case, there lies the power . . . *Now getting involved.* . . . to . . . to roll back the Dark Ages of Man, forever. Knowledge! Ed . . . u . . . cation! *Giving it an exaggerated French pronunciation.* There's the answer. If we can just get all the facts, compile the data. It's pouring in all the time. Do you realize, at this very minute, as you sit here, there are hundreds, thousands, millions of books coming off the presses of the world? In Canada, Russia, America, Sierra Leone. *Almost crying with joy.* Facts. Facts. And every fact brings us closer and closer to Ultimate Truth. Now we're wanderers in a cave with a candle, no, thousands of candles, but soon we'll find the crack. We'll rip off that roof of rock and let in the Great White Light of Knowledge!

SADIE: *covering her face with her shawl*
No.

MOWCHUK:

No more secrets. Think of it! Already we're taking pictures of the dark side of the moon.

SADIE:

No.

MOWCHUK:

All the shadows burnt away.

SADIE:

No.

MOWCHUK:

No dark corners.

SADIE:

No.

MOWCHUK:

No basements.

SADIE:

No.

MOWCHUK:

No caves.

SADIE:

No.

MOWCHUK:

No jungles.

SADIE:

No.

MOWCHUK:
No bogeymen to come down from the attic and eat you up if you're a bad boy. *Catching himself.* That's how I try to describe it to my students.

SADIE uncovers her face.

SADIE:
You're a teacher. What do you teach, Mowchuk? I said, what do you teach?

MOWCHUK:
I beg your pardon?

SADIE:
Or have you been fired?

MOWCHUK:
No!

SADIE:
Then this is a second job?

MOWCHUK: *French accent again*
Une avocation!

SADIE:
What do you teach?

MOWCHUK: *defensively*
Violin.

SADIE:
I should have guessed. Long sensitive fingers.

MOWCHUK:
Not like that. Music is logic. It's closer to mathematics than the arts. When Man lives by his emotions he's an animal. His intellect makes him God. Not in the orthodox sense, of course. I used to be a Catholic. But I'm

happy to say I've rid myself of that primitive conditioning. Rubbing beads, drinking blood, eating flesh . . . Repulsive, even symbolically. And these men go out to convert! While actually it's people like me knocking at doors like yours . . .

SADIE:
You think I need converting? Why me, Mowchuk? Why my house?

MOWCHUK: *flustered*
I had a list.

SADIE:
You think you've come by chance? Talk. I want you to talk, but about Leonard Mowchuk. Not what he's representing.

MOWCHUK:
But that's not . . . They didn't send me out here to . . .

SADIE:
Oh yes, they did.

MOWCHUK:
I . . . I can't. I won't! I won't give myself . . . myself . . . away so . . . so . . .

SADIE:
You force me to be blunt, Muffett.

MOWCHUK:
Mowchuk. Leonard Mowchuk . . .

SADIE:
A woman doesn't enjoy that. I'm not sure I'll forgive you. You are a salesman and I am a buyer. "A relationship." There aren't many of those left anymore. Mother and child? Husband and wife? Lovers? *Dismissing each of them.* Hunh! Who cares about me,

unh? You. Why, you and I might be the last two people in the world having a real conversation. Would you care to sit on the couch? *She lifts an edge of the sheet seductively.*

MOWCHUK:
Are you suggesting? . . . I won't . . .

SADIE:
Everything in this world has a flowering, Mowchuk, even those things we think aren't alive. It may be a dance or a glow or a song, like I said, sometimes so short that after it's finished you wonder if you heard it at all. But in this house we have time and time to listen . . .

MOWCHUK:
What . . . do you expect me to do?

SADIE:
Why, have tea, of course. With my friends.

MOWCHUK:
If you'd only let me . . . leave me . . . My head . . .

SADIE: *suddenly realizing*
Why, Leonard Mowchuk, it's . . . your first time. Isn't it. Isn't it? Admit it. It's nothing to be ashamed of. We all have a first.

MOWCHUK nods his head, miserable, unable to look at her.

No wonder he was early, Puss. Anxious, poor Muffett. And incompetent. No, you weren't either. Shame, Sadie Golden. *To MOWCHUK.* It'll get easier and easier, you'll see.

MOWCHUK:
My mind, it's . . . I can't concentrate.

SADIE:
Is your head . . . hurting?

He nods. His inadvertent sounds counterpoint her lines. She approaches his chair from behind.

Close your eyes. It's better you should learn from me . . .

MOWCHUK: *to himself, puzzled*
Tiptop shape, mental and physical . . .

SADIE:
. . . an older woman, more mature and experienced, who can help the situation along with . . . delicacy.

SADIE starts to massage MOWCHUK's head. He jumps.

Don't shrink from me! *He falls back.* I used to do it for my son. *She continues to massage.* A gentle woman, yet one who tells it to you straight, if you make that necessary. Relax! Better. There are other guests coming, but not yet. I can't count how many of them I've introduced to the art of our . . . relationship.

SADIE begins to massage MOWCHUK's shoulders. Again he jumps nervously and subsides.

It won't hurt. I'm not demanding. You'll see. I wish . . . If I'd known . . . I'd of been looking more appropriate. What did I ever ask of my son? Which is what I got, but I'll get more out of you, won't I, Leonard?

MOWCHUK: *almost unconscious*
Name . . . I can't remember . . .

SADIE: *still massaging*
Aren't there . . . aren't there little things, small things, little buts in your mind that you'd like to let fly out? Things you'd like to tell?

MOWCHUK appears to be dozing. His sounds, which have become grunts of submission and pleasure, transform into a light snore. SADIE, furious, shakes him.

SADIE:
Get up! You're here to help.

MOWCHUK: *barely awake*
You want me to . . .

He stumbles to the box. As he starts to push, he becomes aware of what's in it.

SADIE:
That box! Push it to the cupboard. I want something

Advertisements?

She points to a high cupboard drawer.

You're taller than me.

MOWCHUK climbs up on the box.

Reach way in the back.

MOWCHUK: *pulling his hand back, frightened*
Christ! It was warm.

SADIE:
That's my fur jacket, ninny. Behind that.

MOWCHUK:
What did I just say? A profanity! Pardon me, Mrs. Golden.

SADIE:
I've heard worse.

MOWCHUK:

Not that. I'm against overprotecting the female sex. But that I should call on God . . . It's . . . it's unsettling . . . You see, I was brought up as a Catholic, but . . . Or did I mention that?

SADIE: *dryly*

It's at the back of the cupboard, Mr. Mowchuk.

MOWCHUK puts his hand in. He pulls it out again.

MOWCHUK:

Is this absolutely necessary? I feel as though I'm being indiscreet. Reaching into your . . . intimate places. I prefer to see what I'm touching.

SADIE:

Absolutely necessary. It's in a case.

MOWCHUK:

Yes, as I was saying. I'm an atheist now. It's the only logical conclusion a man of intellect can reach. Do you have a rag? Not that I'm suggesting . . .

MOWCHUK is troubled by the dirt and cobwebs. He takes out his hanky to wipe himself before he reaches in again. Eventually his face and clothes are smeared with grime.

What I can't stand are individuals who announce they've "suspended their judgement." Can't be done, you know. One has to choose. Actually they're cowards. *He reaches in again and suddenly screams.* Holy Mother of God. Something moved. *He teeters on the box.*

SADIE:

Are you alright?

MOWCHUK:

I did it again. Did you hear me? Those words. After all these years. Regression. It's this house.

SADIE: *dryly*

It's mice or bats, maybe. Not a Holy Spirit. Mind, they all like dark places. If you'd rather, I'll . . .

MOWCHUK:

No. No. I'm perfectly capable . . .

He reaches up again, closes his eyes, and plunges his arm in. The phone rings. SADIE exits as MOWCHUK pulls out a case.

SADIE:

Hello?

MOWCHUK can't resist a desire to open the case. In it is a violin.

Offstage. Yes, Mr. Applebaum. Three o'clock. And don't forget to bring the flowers.

MOWCHUK:

She's a witch.

SADIE: *re-entering*

Well? You're not playing.

MOWCHUK doesn't answer.

Sadie Golden forces no one to do anything. It was just a silly dream I had. Music for my party would make it like . . . like a salon. Isn't that what they used to call them? Welcome to Sadie's Salon. I bought it for my son, but he won't even spit on it. He's full of music. The few times he played it when he was a kid, everything stood on tiptoe to listen. Now he's . . . Rock'n' Roll.

MOWCHUK: *in spite of himself, he has touched the violin.*

What?

SADIE:

Rock'n'Roll. To aggravate me, he bought a clock radio; he presets it, anytime, in the middle of the night, four in the morning, three in the afternoon, it blares full volume. I never know if it's him upstairs in his room or if it's the clock. Listen.

She goes to the stairway. They listen. Nothing is heard.

He's not home. Or then again, he might be. I told him he's perfectly . . . *She shouts upstairs.* . . . welcome to move out whenever he wants. Maybe he has. Play, Leonard Mowchuk. *Her voice changes suddenly to command.* I said play!

MOWCHUK has wiped the violin with a hanky. He nervously raises it under his chin and starts to play with a definite squeak: "Bye Baby Bunting"

That's it. Beautiful. Maybe you'll reconsider a recital for the guests.

As he plays, SADIE, smiling, drifts into the kitchen. MOWCHUK becomes aware that he's alone.

MOWCHUK:

Where . . . am I? Define. On a floor. Between four . . . three walls and a window. In a house, in fact. Something has gone wrong. Something has definitely . . . it's a dream. How to test it? Pain. With what? Pin. *He takes off his tie pin and jabs it into his arm.* Never give up. The rules. Where's the rule book? No. No cheating. Recite from memory. But they didn't prepare me for anything like . . . Index. Index Manual, that's it. *Getting a book from his briefcase, he flips wildly through the pages.* Encounter problems. They'll have her in here. Babies. No . . . Dogs. No. Husband. No. Pregnancy . . . *He closes the book.* Wasting time. Try again. Rehearse.

He picks up the violin, which is used as a humourous dramatic countervoice, and begins to play long drawn-out screeching notes while reciting and marching back and forth. If this is too difficult, he can pluck the strings, starting and stopping according to the progress of his argument.

Rehearse while she isn't here. Rehearse what? The rules. What rules? She doesn't follow rules. She should go over them, not me. She doesn't act like a client's supposed to. It's not my fault. I did everything I could. Did you? Step number one: Salesman approaches door, shoulders back, chin squared, if possible. Knocks on door . . . Even that. Never mind. No self-pity. Step number two: Greet the customer like an old friend, but with respect . . . She didn't give me a chance. I should be at the Illustration Section by now. Step number three: Casually guide the conversation to topic of mutual interest . . .

No self-pity, Mowchuk! Without making client feel ignorant, tactfully suggest how knowledge can be supplemented by the use of the . . . of the . . . The Universal Books of Knowledge. Step number four: Step number four: . . . Forgotten. *Mumbling, he goes through steps which get more and more disjointed, tempo increasing as he approaches step number four.* Step number one: Approaching door . . . confidence, Leonard Mowchuk. Step number two: Topic of mutual . . . Step number three: Suggest use of books . . . Step number four: My mind's a blank. Nonsense. Impossible. The excuse is unacceptable. You won't take it from students, so why from you? It's strictly a mechanical proposition. The brain is a machine connected by the nervous system to sensory perception nodes. *As though giving a lecture.* Experience is programmed through these nodes of touch, sight, sound and smell to the brain where knowledge is imposed on the grey tissue as firmly as impressions in wax. It can't . . . just . . . disappear. *He starts to play again and pace frantically.* Step number one . . . Step number two . . .

Step three . . . Step four . . . step four . . . *A terrible cry.* Fooour! *Sadly.* It's time for a moment of honesty. It's not that poor woman's fault you're not successful. She wouldn't be able to withstand the vigour of your onslaught if you believed in your mission, but the sad fact is . . . It's not that you can't remember. No, no. It's not that. Question: Do you believe in what you're selling? Answer: I don't know. Question: Do you believe that Mrs. Golden will benefit by The Universal Books of Knowledge? Will she ever read them? Does she need them? Answer: I don't know. I don't know. Question: Do you have a right to be in this house, a right to have the presumption to presume that another human being as compared with yourself is ignorant? Answer: I don't know. Leonard Muffett! You are a failure! I . . . give . . . you . . . zero!

MOWCHUK starts to pack up and leave, but in his confusion he overlooks the Index Manual.

SADIE: *re-entering*
Mr. Mowchuk.

MOWCHUK:
Yes, Mrs. Golden?

SADIE:
Universal Books of Knowledge, isn't it?

MOWCHUK: *hopefully*
Yes, yes it is.

SADIE:
On Main and Hastings?

MOWCHUK:
That's right.

SADIE dials a number.

SADIE:

Hello? Dr. Wiseman please, the local supervisor of the Universal Books of Knowledge. That's right. Sadie Golden here. I'm sorry to hear you're sick, Doctor. You're not? What's wrong, then. I'm not good enough for you to come around yourself nowadays? No. I'm not complaining. There's one of your salesmen here right now. He's doing very well, this young man, Mr. Muffett.

MOWCHUK: *whispers ardently*

Mowchuk.

SADIE:

So far. In fact, I'm thinking of writing a letter to the Head Office about him. He should make you feel nervous. He might take away your job. No, I'm not comparing. I wouldn't do that. But you should keep an eye on him. Shall I phone you later? Or would you rather come by for tea? How is three o'clock?

She hangs up. She checks off WISEMAN's name on her list.

Play more! I wish my son could have heard you just now. He'd have learned a lot. Unfortunately he took after his father. A pig. Not a bad man. Dead. Don't misunderstand me. Decent, honourable, dependable. He adored me. Couldn't keep his hands off . . .

A sudden jangling burst of rock music is heard. SADIE starts to run upstairs, but the phone rings. She runs downstairs and picks up the phone. She shouts.

Hello? Yes. Three o'clock.

She runs upstairs again. While she's climbing the stairs, the front door opens. A huge sack of mail is thrown in. It narrowly misses MOWCHUK. MOWCHUK, distracted now, seizes his coat and briefcase and starts to run out the front door. He trips over the sack of mail. The music stops. SADIE comes back downstairs. She sees MOWCHUK leaving.

So. I might have guessed. It's a good thing I've learned not to trust anyone. I used to be soft. Any fool could take advantage of Sadie Golden. My own family taught me better. I could see right from the beginning what you were, twitching to get out. But you're going to see, it's not so easy now. You opened my door.

MOWCHUK:
It opened itself.

SADIE:
Under the pressure of your knuckles. You're on this side now. Something's begun, Leonard Mowchuk, between you and your chair and Puss and the violin. And me.

MOWCHUK has been listening half hypnotized. A moan is heard from his chair; a sound is heard from the violin. He makes a dash for the door. The sounds stop as he moves.

So? Why aren't you gone? I wouldn't expect you to feel guilty about leaving. You'd walk in my door and out again whhhsshht, just like that, if you could. I'm not sure it'll let you out, but then again he might. I've got a son, Mr. Mowchuk, who shrinks from me when I go to kiss him. What are you standing there for? You're going. "Mind your own business," they tell me. What other business has a mother got to mind? I'll soon be dead and gone. Do you think it's for my sake? I don't count anymore. I used to be beautiful. I watched the veins sprout like grapes on my hips and my breasts when I was pregnant. They share nothing with me, not even their troubles. My hands were spoilt washing diapers. My skin smells from all the meals I cooked for them, herring, cabbage rolls, doughnuts . . . When I lie awake at night I can see the smell rising off me like mist, like the spatter of frying fat. But what do you care? You talk about logical conclusions but you're running away.

MOWCHUK: *concerned*
You . . . You . . . You're distraught. *Trying to touch her shoulder.*

SADIE:
Don't touch me. After you've hurt someone it's no good. You don't touch.

Hard rock music suddenly blares forth again. SADIE rushes up the stairs. The music stops. She re-enters, stands still, and stares fixedly at MOWCHUK. Then, without warning, she slaps him hard. Her love anguish here is real.

My own son, why do you turn away from me? Did I do do something to hurt your feelings? I'm sorry. Did I say too much? I'm sorry. Look how I humble myself. Just let me touch . . . *She reaches out to him.*

MOWCHUK:
I'll stay . . . a little longer.

SADIE: *playing the brave mother*
Why should you? I want you to leave. You must have other appointments. I don't want to force you to do anything you don't want to.

MOWCHUK:
I want to stay. No. Really, I want to.

SADIE:
Are you sure? Puss doesn't believe you.

She picks up the cat and holds her out to MOWCHUK. MOWCHUK strokes her. SADIE smiles, in control. Her voice purrs.

There's my good boy.

act two

DICKENS rings the doorbell. SADIE jumps guiltily.

SADIE:

Hunh! Mr. Dickens. Already. Quick! Into the kitchen.

SADIE throws a sheet over the teacups and the table. MOWCHUK, distracted, obeys each instruction until the next one arrests and redirects him.

No. Behind the couch. No. Under the table. Why are you running around like a fool? Stay in your chair. You twitch, that's your trouble. You're a twitcher. Not Mr. Dickens. There's not a quarter inch of doubt in him.

SADIE takes off her apron. She touches her hair nervously. DICKENS knocks. SADIE rushes into the hall then back again. She pulls the cover off the love-seat, balls it up, throws it behind the sofa, thinks better of it, pulls it out again, and offers an end to MOWCHUK.

Hurry. He's waiting.

MOWCHUK helps her fold the cover.

Put it in the cupboard. No. Behind the couch. Oh my God, what'll he say. Back on the loveseat.

MOWCHUK obeys. DICKENS' knock is followed by a doorbell this time.

Why are you looking so scared? How can you expect others to have confidence in you . . .

She pushes him into his chair, drags the mailbag to one side, rushes to the front door, and opens it to reveal DICKENS, a man in his fifties, big-bellied, with a sonorous, pompous voice, and a British accent. SADIE tries to appear collected.

Mr. Dickens! What a surprise!

DICKENS:
By my watch it is precisely 1:30 p.m. on this day the first Monday of the month. Or am I mistaken in my calculations?

SADIE:
If you're here it must be true.

DICKENS enters and hands SADIE his hat. She puts it on the hallstand. This and the following have been done every month for fifteen years.

DICKENS:
Happening to find myself in the neighborhood it came upon me that I might drop in for a cup of tea.

SADIE:
Mr. Dickens, you didn't just happen . . .

DICKENS:
That was an interminably long interval between my ringing then knocking then knocking ringing and your answering of the door, my dear . . .

SADIE:
I was busy preparing for you.

DICKENS: *looking suspiciously down the hall*
Then it must have been, and I'm sure it was, a mere firmament of my imagination . . .

SADIE:
You have so many of those.

DICKENS:
I perceived, that is, I thought I perceived, as I made my laborious way up your path . . .

SADIE bends to help DICKENS take off his buckle galoshes. He has wide, baggy trousers and a vest under his jacket.

I can't continue. I might rupture something far more precious to me than . . .

SADIE:
You have to. You never leave your sentences unfinished, Mr. Dickens. I'd be thinking all sorts of silly endings.

DICKENS: *abruptly*
A male voice! Impossible, I know, soundwaves of a particular resonance emulating from within your domicile.

SADIE:
Your face, it's quite jaundiced, Mr. Dickens. Have you been unwell?

DICKENS:
Are you trying to disarm me?

SADIE:

You haven't been taking the magnesia I gave you. Am I right? I've told you and told you . . . But where . . . You didn't bring . . . *Disappointed.*

DICKENS:

Be at rest, dear lady. Have I even once during our long relationship forgotten this precious object?

Dramatically, he pulls out his briefcase from under his coat. It's long and narrow, a sample box.

SADIE:

Ooooooh. It's bigger than I remembered.

DICKENS:

Just protecting it in case of rain. I could never replace it, as you well know.

SADIE goes to take it. DICKENS pulls away, shocked.

Not yet!

SADIE: *apologetically*

I don't know what got into me.

DICKENS:

It's usually you who chasticates me.

SADIE:

For being impatient. You're quite right. The pleasure is in the pace. We've discussed it often.

DICKENS:

Not often. We understand each other without . . .

SADIE takes DICKENS' coat. She hangs it up.

SADIE:

You're thinner.

DICKENS: *still suspicious, looking down the hall*
Saving up. I always starve between our visits.

SADIE:
Then you should make them more often.

DICKENS:
A man should show constraint, especially in his pleasures.

They start down the hall. SADIE is getting more nervous and giddy as they go.

SADIE:
You're looking pale. My mint tea will do you good.

DICKENS:
It always does. And you? There's nothing new, I hope?

SADIE:
Mr. Golden, his demands, he's getting worse. *In a half whisper.* You wouldn't believe . . .

A sound is heard from MOWCHUK. DICKENS sees him and stops, confounded. SADIE, enjoying the situation, turns coquette.

Oh, I don't think you two have met. Mr. Mowchuk, this is my dear friend Mr. Dickens. Mr. Dickens, Mr. Mowchuk.

MOWCHUK: *coming forward with his hand proffered*
How do you do?

SADIE: *to DICKENS*
Aren't you going to shake hands? Why are you looking . . . I didn't plan it. I didn't think that he . . . That is, when you . . . Not at the same time.

DICKENS:
Adulteress!

MOWCHUK: *his voice, as at the beginning of the play, has a strange squeak to it.* I can't let you talk to the lady like that.

DICKENS:
You can't . . . let me . . . Pooh . . . Pooh . . . Whoo . . .

DICKENS' cheeks puff in and out like an angry toad. He starts to choke.

I . . . can't . . . breathe . . .

SADIE: *taking some keys off a string around her neck*
Oh dear. Oh dear. He's having an attack. Get wine. Wine, Mr. Mowchuk. In the cabinet. *She throws the keys to MOWCHUK.*

DICKENS: *suddenly observant*
You'd throw him your keys?

As SADIE's attention returns to him, DICKENS returns to sputtering and moaning.

SADIE:
Sit down and rest, my dear Mr. Dickens. It's going to be alright. Sadie Golden will make everything all . . .

Happily hypnotized, DICKENS is almost seated on the loveseat.

Not there! *Harshly.* You've come here often enough.

DICKENS, moaning histrionically, stumbles to another sheeted piece of furniture, pulls off the sheet with his hand behind him, and sinks into large stuffed armchair with footstool, obviously meant for the man of the house.

That's better.

With his eyes closed DICKENS helps SADIE fold the sheet.

DICKENS: *in a moan which continues until he drinks*
Shame shame shame shame shame . . .

SADIE:
Shhh. Don't try to say anything. *To MOWCHUK.* Where's the wine? Idiot! Don't drop it. *She holds the cut glass decanter to DICKENS' lips.* An anniversary gift. From Mr. Golden.

DICKENS sputters.

You've had too much. *She pulls it away.* You'll go to sleep like Golden — when he isn't having me. Everything to satisfy his needs!

DICKENS:
Shame, shame . . . *Then in weak agreement through her following speech.* . . . same, same, same . . .

SADIE: *together with DICKENS' refrain*
But you, you're decent, considerate, honourable, dependable. What would Sadie Golden have done without her Dickens all these years, eh? With only that . . .

DICKENS ends the "same" duet.

. . . toad and his son to hop in and out the door. But the first Monday . . .

DICKENS: *happily, by rote*
. . . of every month . . .

SADIE AND
DICKENS: *together*

. . . for the past fifteen years, Mr. Dickens has come to Sadie Golden.

SADIE stands by DICKENS' chair, as though posing for a photograph. Husband and wife. Tintype style. A twang from the kitchen stove is heard.

SADIE: *exiting to the kitchen*

My turkey!

DICKENS collects his dignity.

DICKENS:

Hmmmmmmm. Haaaa.

A possible interplay of sound here between the two men — throat clearing, bits of humming or whistling.

MOWCHUK:

Just so.

DICKENS:

Just so what?

MOWCHUK:

What you said. Just . . . that.

DICKENS:

Aha! Agreeable. Trying to be agreeable. *He circles MOWCHUK, who pivots as he moves around him.* Not convincing.

MOWCHUK:

UNconvincing.

DICKENS:

DISagreeable.

MOWCHUK:

I didn't mean anything by it. I can't help myself. Correcting people, I mean. It's like a tic. It gets me in all sorts of . . .

DICKENS, while slowly circling MOWCHUK, begins to audibly sniff him like a dog testing his competition.

Does everyone do that here?

DICKENS:

I . . . smell . . . a savage.

MOWCHUK:

I beg your pardon!

DICKENS:

An opportunist, a hoodlum, a hippie . . .

MOWCHUK:

The terms are not interchangeable.

DICKENS: *still circling him*

Ha!

MOWCHUK:

Sir, if I were not in the house of a lady for whom I have an affection . . .

DICKENS:

I would advise you not to use such words ideally.

MOWCHUK:

"Idly." You said "ideally," but I think you . . .

DICKENS:

Think! Think! You've probably been through college, eh? Apprenticeship, the School of Life, what does that mean nowadays? I know your kind. Coming here trying to bedazzle a defenceless woman.

MOWCHUK:
I don't think she's bedazzled. Or defenseless. On the contrary, I . . . *Hopefully.* Do you think I did that?

DICKENS:
Me, sir? What right have I to thoughts, sir? A poor unlettered working man. *A pause.* You're an old friend of the lady's, I presume?

MOWCHUK:
No! That is, I . . . I'm not sure.

DICKENS:
You wouldn't be here . . . on business, would you?

MOWCHUK:
You know, it's very strange, but . . . I . . . didn't mean it to happen, but . . .

DICKENS:
Yes?

MOWCHUK:
I don't have to answer your questions. Who are you anyway?

DICKENS: *bowing*
Stanley Dickens at your service, one who does have the honour of being an old and trusted friend of the lady of the house.

MOWCHUK:
I already know that much.

DICKENS: *shocked*
She told you about me? *To himself.* Not that too. To sit here and gossip with some . . . *To MOWCHUK.* Did she . . . Did she ask you . . . to . . . sit on the couch?

SADIE: *calling out*
I'll be right with you, gentlemen.

DICKENS:
Damn it, man, how did you get in here?

MOWCHUK:
I walked in.

DICKENS:
You . . .

MOWCHUK:
The door opened itself. Of course I don't believe in ghosts . . .

DICKENS: *relieved*
Walked in. Without knocking, I presume.

MOWCHUK:
Or assume, though neither actually . . .

DICKENS: *drawing himself up pompously*
Friendship, Mr. . . .

MOWCHUK:
Mowchuk. Leonard Mowchuk. *Again, he offers him his hand, which is ignored.*

SADIE peeks through the kitchen hatch.

DICKENS:
. . . involves certain moral obligations.

MOWCHUK:
That's something I understand.

DICKENS:
Mrs. Golden is a naive, one might even say, gullible woman.

SADIE smiles. The hatch closes.

DICKENS:
I'm not discrediting her. These are rare virtues. There are some who might try to take advantage.

MOWCHUK:
I can't tell you how pleased I . . . how pleased I am to meet you. *He comes forward, seizes DICKENS' hand and pumps it.* Mowchuk. Leonard Mowchuk. It's not often one comes across a man with a social conscience.

DICKENS:
Let go, pup. *Disentangling himself.* I can see as well as anyone else what you're after. I'll tell you straight. I intend to protect her from you.

MOWCHUK:
My intentions are the best, sir.

DICKENS:
You will have no intentions, sir. How did you get here? By car? I didn't see any car at the curb. By bus? Go on, admit it. And you paid for two seats, am I right? For you and that puny valise, eh? A greener, an amateur, wet behind the ears . . . That Lincoln is my car, sir! *Pointing outside.* Be warned!

SADIE enters, smiling innocently.

SADIE:
Well, gentlemen. How are you getting on? Friends already, I can tell. Have you said hello to Puss yet, Mr. Dickens? She'll think you're angry with her. You wouldn't want that, would you?

SADIE picks up the cat and holds it out to DICKENS.

Would you, Mr. Dickens?

Reluctantly, DICKENS pats the cat, avoiding MOWCHUK's eyes.

DICKENS: *taking her to one side*
Why didn't you explain? He took advantage of your good nature. You must learn how to fend off rascals, my dear. Or the little rats, they'll go nibble nibble . . .

SADIE: *momentarily hard*
And there'd be no cheese left for you. *Warmly again, loud enough for MOWCHUK to hear.* Silly man! I'd have told you I was innocent if you'd given me the chance. It's that jealousy of yours. Don't deny it. Sometimes it scares me. *A pleasurable fear.* I lie awake beside Golden listening to the night noises . . .

DICKENS: *an anxious whisper*
Not in front of . . . *Pompously, to MOWCHUK.* You will leave now, Mr. Whatever-your-name-is . . .

MOWCHUK:
I'll leave when the lady asks me.

DICKENS:
Well? One word. *He whispers.* Our time together, madam.

MOWCHUK: *almost to himself*
I've been trying all afternoon to get out. Now it seems a question of honour that I stay.

SADIE:
He stays.

DICKENS:
Wha . . . I'm . . . I . . .

The beginning of another collapse. DICKENS looks to see if SADIE is fetching the wine. She isn't, but MOWCHUK rushes to pour a glass. DICKENS ignores him.

I'm speechless.

SADIE:
Hardly.

DICKENS:
Can this be my Mrs. Golden? And this The House?

SADIE:
Why are you upset?

DICKENS:
There are certain things . . . certain things in life one ought to be able to depend on. Out there . . . *He gestures to the window.* Vicious. A fight against billboards and television and God knows what next . . .

SADIE:
You're getting excited again. Sit down.

DICKENS:
It's one way streets and red lights and who believes in God, eh? A man takes a step he might sink out of sight. But the rest of them keep right on walking.

SADIE eases DICKENS into the armchair and lifts his feet onto the footstool.

SADIE:
There, there. I almost have a mind to send Muffet away . . . *She looks at MOWCHUK.* No.

DICKENS: *relaxing back in his chair*
But here, this room, you . . .

SADIE:
Shhhhhh.

DICKENS:
Something a man could hold onto. A plateau, an oasis, no, no, more, a faith.

MOWCHUK:
That's blasphemy.

SADIE gestures impatiently for him to be silent.

DICKENS:
Did somebody . . .

SADIE:
Shhh. The first . . .

DICKENS:
Monday . . .

SADIE:
Of every month . . .

DICKENS:
By my watch it is precisely 1:30 p.m. . . .

While speaking in a singsong voice. SADIE tucks in DICKENS with the sheet from his chair.

SADIE:
Good afternoon, Mr. Dickens.

DICKENS:
Finding myself in the neighbourhood . . .

SADIE:
Come in. You're looking pale . . .

DICKENS:
Saving up between visits.

SADIE:
Then you should come . . .

SADIE AND DICKENS: *sung together, as in a religious ritual*
More often.

DICKENS: *with a beatific childlike smile*
Like in a holy place. *He closes his eyes.*

SADIE: *singing*
Aamen. *To MOWCHUK, who has risen.* Shhhhh.

Gesturing to him, SADIE leads the way toward the kitchen. DICKENS wakes with a start.

DICKENS:
Where're you going?

SADIE:
To let you rest.

DICKENS: *suspiciously*
What were you going to do in there?

SADIE:
Why, Mr. Dickens. You *are* jealous.

DICKENS:
Of him? Ha! I'm jealous *for* you, not *of* you. Ha! Poof.

MOWCHUK: *embarrassed*
I'm intruding.

DICKENS:
You finally noticed.

MOWCHUK:
Mrs. Golden, if you don't mind . . .

DICKENS: *exploding*
If it'd been me I wouldn't have had to pay for my sample case. The bus driver would have begged me to let it ride free.

MOWCHUK:
That's dishonest. Well, isn't it? How do I know *you're* not taking advantage of Mrs. Golden?

DICKENS: *starting to circle MOWCHUK*
What do you sell?

MOWCHUK:
Books. *He starts to move.*

DICKENS: *with exaggerated disbelief*
Books?

MOWCHUK: *defensively*
Books. And you?

DICKENS:
Condiments.

SADIE: *delighted*
Gentlemen! My goodness, are you going to fight over me?

They circle each other, the female forgotten in preparation for the dog fight.

As the men argue. SADIE drags a large piece of furniture covered with a sheet to stage centre. She places Puss at her right hand.

MOWCHUK: *genuinely incredulous*
You mean food?

DICKENS:
Sustenance, I mean.

SADIE:
It's time for our chair, Puss.

She takes off the sheet, revealing an intricately-carved throne chair, perhaps mounted on a small dias, and majestically seats herself, still unnoticed by the jousters. Their lines continue through her action.

DICKENS:
Stimulation, I mean, for the palate.

MOWCHUK:
Frivolities! This . . . *He picks up a book which gives him security.* . . . is necessary.

SADIE smiles.

DICKENS:
Can you smell it, hmmmmm? Taste it, hmmmmm? Eat it?

SADIE:
I shall be She for Whom the Battle Rages. I feel quite giddy.

SADIE hits the cat. A surprisingly resonant note is heard. This is how she registers a hit. There are two notes, one for each man.

MOWCHUK:
Yes, yes, you can. I've got you there. Books feed the mind.

SADIE:
A hit for Mowchuk.

DICKENS:
Arrowroot!

SADIE:
A hit for Dickens.

MOWCHUK:
Anthropology.

SADIE: *indifferently*
Does it hurt, Puss?

SADIE continues to register the hits on Puss throughout the following.

DICKENS:
Basil!

MOWCHUK:
Biology!

DICKENS:
Cardamom!

MOWCHUK:
Cardiology.

DICKENS doubles over, grabbing at his chest. SADIE bangs out the count of nine for a knockdown. DICKENS recovers just in time.

DICKENS: *now on the attack again*
Hunky! What did your father do, eh? Harnessed your mother to a plow to raise potatoes.

MOWCHUK:
You w . . . wasp! You beerbellied de . . . d . . . decadent . . . *Groping for an adequate insult.* . . . Englishman!

DICKENS:
Pope lover!

MOWCHUK:
Convert! Exploiter!

DICKENS:
Job stealer! Immigrant!

MOWCHUK:
Imperialist!

DICKENS:
Communist!

SADIE: *grandly*
My men! You've battled well for me.

A climax of sound, then a sudden silence. The men look around, bewildered, having forgotten SADIE in the excitement of the fight.

For me, yes. And for Puss. She's gone to sleep. One day you'll miaow, won't you, Puss? And the world will go deaf. *To the men.* But you were both entertaining.

SADIE goes to MOWCHUK. She speaks so that DICKENS can't hear.

Your first time? I could hardly believe it. *Referring to DICKENS.* Poor man! I had to comfort him. You understand. So whatever I say . . .

SADIE approaches DICKENS. She speaks so that MOWCHUK can't hear.

You didn't really believe he was here as a . . . That I kept him here to . . . *She laughs freely, clearly.* Look at him! Can a rabbit lock horns with a stag? Aren't you ashamed of yourself?

DICKENS: *appeased somewhat*
He is pathetic.

SADIE:
I stopped keeping points halfway through. I didn't want to embarrass him. *A pause for effect.* It's his first time.

MOWCHUK: *who has been edging in to hear*
Did you have to tell?

DICKENS: *embarrassed for MOWCHUK*
It wasn't necessary, after all.

SADIE pulls DICKENS away from MOWCHUK for a more private conversation.

SADIE:
You have a duty, Mr. Dickens, to teach the apprentice.

DICKENS stares at SADIE uncomprehendingly.

This poor young man needs you. Us.

They look at MOWCHUK. MOWCHUK tries to disappear.

He doesn't know about the subtlety of a relationship such as ours.

MOWCHUK: *now feeling quite paranoid, in an outburst*
I'll not be talked . . . talked . . . talked about like a piece of goods. I w . . . w . . . won't!

SADIE:
You see? He's not mature. He needs an example.

DICKENS:
Are you attempting to humiliate me? I should walk out and leave you open to any little pedlar who . . .

SADIE:
Better he should learn from us, with style, not one two and that's that, thank you very much, the way they do it nowadays. Consider yourself his father.

DICKENS: *raising his arm*
If I were, I'd whip the . . .

SADIE:
Duty is duty.

DICKENS:
For God's sake, Madam.

SADIE:
Your Anglican blood is showing, Mr. Dickens. Look how accommodating he is. He's disappearing into his training chair.

DICKENS: *whispering*
I beg of you . . .

SADIE is silent.

Our product speaks for itself.

SADIE:
I don't hear it.

DICKENS:
In the kitchen. If *he* went in the kitchen maybe . . .

SADIE:
Our boy, a Peeping Tom? What if he got nervous and lost the keyhole at the crucial moment? He wouldn't be able to hear well either. He'd imagine all sorts of things. He has a peculiar imagination, fed on books and lectures, he told me himself. He might even think we . . . *She whispers.*

DICKENS: *giggling, titillated*
Do you think so? *He clears his throat.* Out of the question. I couldn't be natural, knowing he was there.

SADIE:
You could! You could! You have such strong instinct.

SADIE reaches for his briefcase.

DICKENS:
Have you no modesty?

DICKENS stands protectively in front of his sample case.

SADIE:
Then I won't look. And I won't touch.

DICKENS is defeated.

We'll begin with our talk. Side by side as we always do. No? From the loveseat.

SADIE takes one end of the sheet covering the loveseat. then waits for DICKENS to take the other to help her fold. DICKENS stays her hand.

DICKENS:
I can't.

SADIE, with the sheet draped seductively over her and trailing behind, goes to MOWCHUK for folding.

SADIE:
Very well, then. Leonard and I will.

DICKENS:
Leonard? I thought you prided yourself on your style, Madam.

SADIE:
We were almost ready for the couch. *Still trying to persuade DICKENS.* It'll make it more exciting, Mr. Dickens. An extra plum in the pot, huh?

DICKENS:
Voyeurism! I have to revisit my conception of you.

MOWCHUK: *weakly*
Revise. He meant . . .

DICKENS:
You see?

SADIE: *warning*
Muffett, don't be naughty.

DICKENS:
I'm leaving.

DICKENS waits for SADIE to say something. She doesn't. He picks up his briefcase. He expects her to call to him. She doesn't.

I said I'm leaving. I can't be expected to stay on under these conditions.

SADIE:
Goodbye.

DICKENS:
Just like that? That's all?

SADIE:
I've never forced anyone to remain in my house.

DICKENS:
Deny if you can that you're meeting this . . . whelp . . . that you intend . . . for the same purpose you and I . . .

SADIE:
Is it so terrible what you and I do?

DICKENS starts into the hall.

Mr. Dickens!

He turns back hopefully.

I believe I owe you some money. How much?

DICKENS:
Are my ears deceiving me? Such words have never passed between us.

SADIE:
What would you prefer? Cheque or cash?

DICKENS:
Are you driving me to murder, woman?

MOWCHUK rushes up to him.

MOWCHUK:
Don't touch her.

DICKENS hits him. MOWCHUK falls.

DICKENS:
See what you've done? *To SADIE.* You've turned me into a ruffian.

SADIE: *calmly*
Well. You won't be coming back again, will you? Once a tradition is broken . . . It's what you've been thinking. Confess!

DICKENS nods his head, miserable.

Well, how shall it be? Cheque or . . . ? *She wrenches off the cat's head and digs into its belly.* Let me see, I owe you for . . .

DICKENS sobs.

Did you say something? Oh, dear, we only seem to have small change. Hold out your hand. *Loudly.* I said hold . . . *A sweet voice again, counting into his hand.* Five, eight-fifty, ten, fourteen, fourteen-fifty. seventy-five, eighty-five, ninety-five, ninety-six, ninety-seven, ninety-eight, ninety-nine, fifteen. There.

DICKENS:
But I always leave you with credit.

SADIE:
Oh, and five dollars more. For loyal reliable service.

DICKENS: *with dignity*
I don't take tips, Mrs. Golden.

SADIE:
It's your Christmas bonus. I forgot to give it to you.

DICKENS:
You gave me a pudding.

SADIE:
Next year's. I believe that clears the account.

DICKENS:
For God's sake, Sadie . . . *He realizes his unaccustomed familiarity.* I mean, Mrs. . . . *He stumbles into the hall.*

SADIE: *calling after him in a hard voice*
What's the matter? Not enough? Then send me the bill.

MOWCHUK:
Really, Mrs. Golden, I know it's not my place, but . . .

SADIE is listening for the door. DICKENS has paused in front of it. Both of them are breathing heavily. DICKENS opens the door and lets it close again. Pushing MOWCHUK roughly out of her way, SADIE rushes into the hall.

SADIE:
Dickens!

She bumps into DICKENS who is coming back into the living room. They fall against each other. She holds him. All this is ludicrous, but at the same time, poignant.

There. I knew you couldn't leave me. Who knows what horrible things that man might have done? How would you have felt?

MOWCHUK looks around for "that man."

DICKENS: *almost a gasp*
I'm back.

SADIE:
We'll carry on just as we always have.

They go back to their own chairs.

Have you had a good month?

DICKENS nods.

DICKENS: *still speaking with difficulty*
And you?

SADIE:
Mr. Golden, he's getting worse.

DICKENS:
One must be brave.

SADIE:
When I gave birth I bled something awful.

They're both seated now.

DICKENS:
Blessed is he who . . .

SADIE:
The doctor nearly passed out. He said he'd never seen so much blood. My mother warned me.

DICKENS:
Life is difficult.

SADIE:
Giving life.

DICKENS:
You're too generous. You have to learn to hold back.

SADIE: *coming out of the ritual*
Your next part louder. Be natural.

DICKENS: *rising*
How can I? With that foreigner spying.

MOWCHUK starts to move. SADIE beckons him to stay where he is.

SADIE:
Start from the door. It'll be easier for you.

DICKENS, on his way to the hat rack, passes SADIE. She pushes him so the two of them proceed almost at a run.

As she hands him his hat and coat. Hat. Coat. *She opens the door and pushes him out.* Out. *She slams the door.*

DICKENS: *re-entering*
By my watch it is exactly . . .

SADIE:
Your face! If I saw that I'd have a heart attack.

DICKENS adjusts his face.

SADIE hangs up his coat. That's better.

DICKENS:
Happening to find myself in the . . .

SADIE:
You didn't just . . . *She takes DICKENS' hat from him and hangs it up.*

DICKENS:
A man should show constraint . . .

SADIE:
Let me . . .

DICKENS:
There's nothing new, I trust?

They approach the living room at double speed, like a fast moving motion picture film.

SADIE:
It's Golden, you wouldn't believe it.

DICKENS hesitates for just a moment before he enters the living room. SADIE hurriedly puts a sheet on his chair so that he can lift it off. He does.

Sit down. You must be tired.

DICKENS:
One must be brave.

SADIE:
He lay on me last night.

DICKENS:
Blessed is he who learns through . . .

SADIE:
His demands are . . .

DICKENS:
Suffering . . .

SADIE:
Shall I tell you?

DICKENS: *referring to MOWCHUK*
He's in too close.

SADIE:
. . . Getting worse.

DICKENS:
It's a shame that . . .

SADIE:
You wouldn't believe how he . . .

DICKENS: *sitting, though still not relaxed*
Poor good Mrs. Dickens.

SADIE:
Dickens!

DICKENS:
I meant Golden.

SADIE:
You said Dickens.

DICKENS:
A slip of the tongue.

SADIE:
I'm an old tree.

DICKENS:
Not true. Blessed is she who learns through . . .

SADIE:
A dried tree. Use me for firewood. At least then someone could warm their hands by . . .

DICKENS:
Sadie Golden, Sadie Golden.

SADIE:
Or bury me as I am. I might make good fertilizer. A petunia bush from my forehead, a spray of roses from . . . Your spray didn't work.

DICKENS: *showing new interest*
What spray?

SADIE:
For the couch.

DICKENS:
The stain?

SADIE:
Still there.

DICKENS:
I'm glad.

SADIE:
You're wicked.

DICKENS moves to the loveseat and attempts to pull the sheet off it. The sheet, as though animated, resists and returns to its place.

DICKENS:
It won't come off.

SADIE:
Too fast. You're rushing it.

The loveseat, on casters, skitters away from DICKENS.

You men are all the same.

DICKENS pursues the loveseat and stops it. SADIE returns to the ritual. Her following line is the cue for DICKENS to remove the sheet.

SADIE:
Golden beat me.

DICKENS: *sympathetically, yet titillated*
No!

SADIE: *folding the sheet together*
A brute. No culture. Not like you. Right after dinner. I was so tired.

DICKENS:
He beat you?

SADIE:
Wife, mother, cook, all of us . . .

They sit on the loveseat. Rhythm and intimacy intensify.

DICKENS:
I shall be forced to . . .

SADIE:
Last night he . . .

DICKENS:
If I were here I would have . . .

SADIE:
I know you would. But how much? That's the question.

DICKENS:
Don't you trust me?

SADIE:
I'm not sure I trust me. One's own body. Sometimes my stomach, without notifying me at all . . . And my breasts . . .

DICKENS:
A defenceless woman. I'll confront him.

SADIE:
Yes.

DICKENS:
I'll walk up to the door and knock . . .

SADIE:
Hard.

DICKENS: *in a deep voice, as if speaking to her husband*
"What did you mean by . . ."

SADIE:
He's a big man. He'll kill you. He suspects.

DICKENS: *his voice growing suspicious*
Are you? Are you unfaithful?

SADIE: *whispering*
It's time.

They rush to the couch and tear off its sheet, throwing it anywhere.

When you come . . . after you come . . . I feel I'm growing pregnant until the next . . .

DICKENS:
The first Monday . . .

SADIE:
Nobody listens anymore. Nobody cares.

DICKENS:
We do.

They sit on the couch.

SADIE:
Yes. You and I. The last strongholds.

DICKENS:
Civilization.

MOWCHUK looks surprised. They are words similar to those he's heard about himself.

SADIE:
My breasts are heavy.

DICKENS: *looking at his watch*
Soon it will be . . .

SADIE:
Three o'clock. The glare. After I weaned them they didn't stop filling, but no one drinks. Is nobody thirsty?

DICKENS rises.

DICKENS: *urgently*
Faster.

SADIE:
They need me. They couldn't get along without me. I could die and nobody'd notice. Except the dandelions would spread onto the neighbour's lawns. Then they'd come knocking.

DICKENS: *nervous, whispering*
You're changing the order. Not today.

SADIE: *building the pace*
I'd lie here festering, a corpse of love. My children love me. They won't leave me alone. Then they'd feel sorry. My breasts hurt. They'd touch me, the little children, the mothers, the businessmen, the doctors, the plumbers, the dogs would have a sniff too,

and they'd all catch the plague. *She laughs again, a surprisingly clear laughter.* Because that's what happens to milk. It turns rancid. *She looks at DICKENS then screams* ... You weren't listening! I should make you go back to the first chair.

DICKENS: *frightened*
I was! I swear!

SADIE:
I'm a dead tree. Brittle. Birds don't light on me. Cats don't climb.

DICKENS strolls around the room pretending to make a casual study.

DICKENS:
Such a pleasant house.

SADIE:
I'm a husk.

DICKENS:
Order. Everything the same.

SADIE:
My fruit has fallen from me, rotted.

DICKENS: *hissing*
It's nearly time. *He changes his voice.* It never changes. The sideboard, the dining table, the telephone . . .

He puts his hands behind his back and feigns a casualness to mask his excitement.

SADIE:
I curse my daughter! Not even a phone call and a how-do-you-do? Let her love her children like I love her.

DICKENS: *excitement rising*
. . . the cat, the footstool, my armchair.

SADIE:

Bit by bit, stone by stone, let her take away the foundations of her soul and plant them in her children. In the night when she puts her hand on their forehead let it be her forehead. It will be her body she covers in the night. Her ears will be on them. Her arms and her hair will be to protect them from the sun. Then one day let her be surprised when she looks at herself and sees there's nothing left of her but the skin.

She sings.

Bye baby bunting,
Mama's gone a-hunting,
She's taken off her own white skin
To wrap her baby bunting in . . .

DICKENS:

God, I can't wait. Hurry!

SADIE rushes to his briefcase and opens it. DICKENS moans. He is separate from her, never looking directly at what she is doing.

Coriander, basil, sweetbreads, wine, vinegar, lemon . . .

As SADIE touches or strokes each bottle, DICKENS reacts. With a wrench she uncorks a bottle of white fluid. DICKENS squeals.

Floor spray, window spray, hair spray . . .

SADIE drinks from the bottle. The fluid drips over her chin and onto the case. Having satisfied DICKENS, she tosses the bottle behind her. A swoosh of the remaining liquid is heard. MOWCHUK's case opens. He reacts automatically. Books, pamphlets and order forms come out on the floor. MOWCHUK's eyes, like DICKENS', are glazed.

SADIE: *with mock concern*

Oh, dear, I've spilled it.

DICKENS:

I . . . I'll use my handkerchief. *But he doesn't move from where he's sprawled exhausted.*

SADIE:

There, Mr. Dickens, that wasn't so difficult, was it! *She eyes him.* You're out of shape.

DICKENS: *still breathless*

For God's sake, close it up. *He staggers to his case.*

SADIE: *starting towards Puss*

Shall I . . .

DICKENS:

I'll send a bill!

SADIE:

You're right. I'm indiscreet. *She speaks to MOWCHUK on her way.* Naughty boy. Wasted. *The phone rings. She takes it into the kitchen.*

DICKENS is bowed over his briefcase. MOWCHUK, terribly embarrassed, scoops and shoves his material back into his case.

DICKENS: *softly, to himself*

The . . . humiliation.

SADIE: *in the kitchen*

Hello.

MOWCHUK:

Uncalled for. I apologize. I couldn't help myself.

SADIE: *offstage*

My letter meant what it said, Mr. Underhill.

DICKENS:

She wrote to him?

MOWCHUK:
I can't . . .

DICKENS motions to him to be quiet.

SADIE: *offstage*
Premature? I don't think so.

DICKENS:
Jezebel!

SADIE: *offstage*
One must plan for every eventuality. Isn't that your motto? At three o'clock then.

A doubt plagues DICKENS. He goes to the table and lifts a corner of the sheet covering the tea things.

Underhill . . . coming.

MOWCHUK discovers he has left a book out that has been doused by SADIE's bottle.

MOWCHUK: *running to the book*
My book! She's spilled . . . *He tries to wipe off the stain with his hanky, but it is black with dirt from the cupboard.* Your . . . essence on my book.

SADIE: *calling from the kitchen*
I'll be right with you, gentlemen. *Coyly.* When you're ready. One must allow a decent amount of time.

MOWCHUK:
Pages 1365-66, "Rodents in South America," ruined.

DICKENS:
She probably won't even pay for it.

MOWCHUK:
I begin to think . . . I'm forced to say . . . the lady is not as gracious as . . . as we . . .

DICKENS:
Mr. Mowchuk, we must unite. She's united us already in dishonour.

MOWCHUK stares uncomprehending.

To sell, man. That's what we're here for.

MOWCHUK:
Why don't we just leave?

DICKENS:
An eye for an eye . . . We'll sell her till she's busted, the old biddy. To think of the years I . . . She probably can't even read.

MOWCHUK:
Or tell sweet from sour.

They giggle. DICKENS puts his arm around MOWCHUK.

DICKENS:
And I hit you.

MOWCHUK:
I deserved it. I learned a lot from you.

DICKENS:
Did you? You weren't half bad yourself. In fact, you were quite good.

MOWCHUK:
Was I?

DICKENS:
For the first time .

MOWCHUK breaks away from DICKENS.

MOWCHUK:
I can't do it.

DICKENS:
Why not?

MOWCHUK:
My conscience.

DICKENS:
What's conscience got to do with it? We don't owe her anything.

MOWCHUK:
It's like a hairshirt. Up to now I've thought of myself as a Crusader of a kind.

DICKENS:
Who made you doubt it? It is our arduistic task, Mr. Mowchuk, to enrich the life of that ignorant woman. It's your duty.

MOWCHUK:
Enlightenment?

DICKENS:
Who are the teachers in the contemporary world, tell me that?

MOWCHUK: *beginning to pace*
Yes, yes, you inspire me. One relationship, the symbol of an age. For the Greeks it was philosopher and student. For the Romans: Emperor and soldier. For the Christians: Priest and penitent. And now . . .

DICKENS:
Salesman and . . .

MOWCHUK:
Client.

They embrace.

DICKENS:
But remember, we maintain control. We will not be ordered around. We will not turn against each other.

SADIE peeks through the hatch. DICKENS grasps MOWCHUK's arm.

Stay firm?

MOWCHUK:
Stay firm.

DICKENS:
No undercutting?

MOWCHUK:
No undercutting.

DICKENS:
Friendship?

MOWCHUK:
Friendship.

SADIE: *re-entering*
Gentlemen, I must apologize for my clumsiness.

DICKENS:
Perfectly alright, Mrs. Golden.

MOWCHUK:
Don't think any more of it.

SADIE:
Of course I'll pay for the bottle and the book.

DICKENS:
It's just a piffle.

MOWCHUK: *in unison with DICKENS' last line*
I wouldn't dream of it.

DICKENS:
After you, Mr. Mowchuk . . .

MOWCHUK:
No, you, Mr. . .

A shadow is visible at the window.

SADIE: *a sudden command*
Down on your knees!

MOWCHUK drops automatically.

DICKENS:
I will not. *To MOWCHUK.* Fool!

SADIE:
Dickens!

Slowly DICKENS lowers himself to his knees. The shadow crosses.

SADIE squeals with excitement. Oh! Oh! Oh! *She crawls quickly along the floor and hides under a piece of furniture.* Sssst. *She beckons the others to follow.* He can see us. He can see us.

HIGHRISE's extravagantly tall shadow crosses and re-crosses the stage. Laughing to herself, SADIE scurries to hide under the dining room table, pulling the sheet down to cover her. Some teacups crash.

He's coming.

MOWCHUK:
Who is it? Her husband?

DICKENS:
Oh my God!

SADIE: *hissing*
Hide.

More teacups crash. DICKENS dives under his chair.

MOWCHUK: *crawling quickly to join DICKENS*
I thought he was dead.

DICKENS:
Find your own place!

MOWCHUK scurries to his training chair. Bottoms and legs sprout absurdly from between the chair rungs.

HIGHRISE: *offstage*
Fee . . . Fi . . . Fo . . . Fum . . .

HIGHRISE enters with slow strides, his back to the audience. A tall, handsome, flashy man, beginning to show age, perhaps already covering it with make-up, he's dressed in a cape, carrying a cane, and has a hat which is tipped at the back of his head. He is a combination of magic man, aging actor and cheap con. He wears heavy built-up shoes, similar to those used by Greek actors, or, as originally conceived, he's wearing stilts. He looms above the characters and the furniture.

I smell the blood of Sadie Golden. *He sniffs and looks around the room.*

act three

A hysterical giggle is heard from SADIE.

HIGHRISE:
Come out, come out, wherever you are . . .

HIGHRISE reaches out with his cane and lifts the sheet on the table, revealing SADIE curled up covering her eyes.

Or I'll huff and I'll puff . . .

SADIE opens her eyes. The pleasant fright of a child. She covers her eyes again.

You can't hide from Highrise.

SADIE rises slowly from under the dining room table. She takes a few tentative steps towards HIGHRISE, then runs to him. He picks her up and swings her in the air.

Sadie, baby, how are you? You've been preparing for me. You know Jack Highrise. A thousand cups and he's still thirsty. But not just tea, eh?

DICKENS:
It's more than you she's expecting.

HIGHRISE:
What's this? Do you suffer, madam, from crawling . . . *He removes the chair from DICKENS.* . . . insects? Look, it's a toad, and here . . . *He tries to take the chair from MOWCHUK, but he holds onto it.* . . . a turtle. *Wrenching the chair away.* Without its shell. Embarrassing to see a turtle without a shell. Makes you want to . . . *He rises high on one foot.* . . . end its misery.

SADIE:
No!

HIGHRISE:
Are they friends of yours?

SADIE:
Why not? Why should it be only you who . . .

DICKENS: *standing*
Who . . . who is this man? I demand to know . . . All these years you made me think . . .

HIGHRISE:
Toads don't think. They croak. Croak, toad. *He holds his came to DICKENS' throat.*

DICKENS:
What's in that thing?

HIGHRISE:
Adjustable, moves in and out. Croak.

DICKENS opens his mouth and croaks. MOWCHUK opens his mouth and croaks too.

Not you, fool. You chirp.

MOWCHUK chirps.

SADIE:
I used to have a pet toad. Two of them. At the summer beach cottage. They'd hop every morning to my bedroom to be fed. Here, little toads.

HIGHRISE:
Hop! Hop!

DICKENS hops to SADIE. MOWCHUK follows.

SADIE:
They would sit in my lap . . .

DICKENS stops. HIGHRISE gestures with his cane. DICKENS croaks, hops and sits in SADIE's lap. Kept at a distance by HIGHRISE, MOWCHUK's longing chirps breaks into . . .

MOWCHUK:
Me too . . . me too . . . me too . . .

SADIE:
I fed them milk. *She unbuttons her blouse.*

DICKENS:
It's beyond . . .

HIGHRISE gestures again. A knife shoots out of his cane. DICKENS buries his head against SADIE's breasts. Sucking sounds are heard.

SADIE:

Every morning they came . . .

MOWCHUK, not to be kept back now, hopping and chirping, nestles against SADIE.

One, of course, turned into a prince, but I threw him away. *She shoves MOWCHUK away.* Sometimes the ants would come.

HIGHRISE mimes this and provides the sounds.

They didn't frighten me.

MOWCHUK patters back in a new guise.

Slugs would leave trails that looked like dance patterns with me at the centre. And the birds. Down from the trees they flew.

HIGHRISE makes flying, chirping, and other appropriate sounds.

I had lots of milk for all of them. No. Don't fight. Some of them nibbled at the tips of my fingers. Or my ears. But they grew back. You see, there were no leaves in the forest, no worms, no berries, just me. When I left, every autumn it was the same. I could hear the birds behind me fall out of their nests out of the trees . . . kerplunk, kerplunk . . .

HIGHRISE takes over the dull thud sound.

. . . from hunger.

SADIE stands up. DICKENS rolls out of her lap. MOWCHUK falls from her shoulder.

All dead.

DICKENS:
No. No.

HIGHRISE grinds his cane into DICKENS.

SADIE:
Without me.

HIGHRISE: *to SADIE*
Hey. Bravo. Better than you've ever done it.

DICKENS: *weakly, as he sits up*
I thought I was . . .

HIGHRISE:
Rubber, idiot. Look.

HIGHRISE jabs at MOWCHUK who tries to evade him. MOWCHUK cuts his hand.

Sorry.

SADIE:
Shame on you, Jack Highrise. Mommy'll make it better.
She rushes out for a bandage.

HIGHRISE:
Ant, turtle, toad? Between us, gentlemen, we're all the same, leeches, including out dear . . . hostess.

HIGHRISE, taking off his shoes as he talks, gestures to the door where SADIE enters.

SADIE: *bringing bandages for MOWCHUK*
To HIGHRISE. You are a wicked man, Highrise. I don't know why I let you in the house. But you'll all learn to love each other.

DICKENS:
How much have you given this man? I've a right to know.

HIGHRISE:

Is this your husband? I thought he was dead. I read a notice in the obituaries, and I said to myself, "Sadie Golden needs me. For her pleasures. She'll be able to afford them again. What luck I'm ready for her."

SADIE:

Are you?

DICKENS:

Dead? You didn't tell me.

SADIE:

Well, Highrise? The shoes and the stick weren't bad, as an entrance. But what have you really brought me today?

HIGHRISE: *going into a spiel*

Bricks, Incorporated. Special interlocking bricks that need no cement, no nails, no design. They interlock themselves and you don't know what you're building, ladies and gentlemen, until it's built itself around you. The trick is, it builds according to what's enclosed. A demonstration. Free of charge, my friends. *He mimes setting up a machine, making the appropriate sounds.* For you, my fair Fury . . . *To SADIE.* A castle with a grand salon. My bricks interlock themselves into people too, who laugh precisely when you want, and when you want, shut up. You don't like someone? Why, take him apart. *He mimes demolition.* For you . . . *To MOWCHUK.* A monk's cell, with a nun of bricks. Hard to make, but dependable. And for you . . . *To DICKENS.* An interlocking shithouse. *Mimicking DICKENS sitting in his chair as if it were a toilet.* "Let me comfort you. Stiff upper lip. One learns through suffering."

SADIE:

Not interested. What else?

HIGHRISE:
I was afraid you'd say that. Fact is, I'm tired.

SADIE: *excited*
Are the police after you?

HIGHRISE:
Tired.

SADIE:
With dogs? I'd love to hear them howling outside the window.

HIGHRISE starts to take off his jacket.

Not yet! Gentlemen wait for a lady's permission to disrobe. *A change in tone.* You may take it off Highrise! You didn't come here to rest, did you?

HIGHRISE: *recovering himself*
How could I, with Sadie Golden? *He takes off his jacket, then his stilts.*

MOWCHUK: *to DICKENS*
His legs! They came off!

DICKENS: *pulling MOWCHUK to one side*
They're stilts.

MOWCHUK: *looking back as he's being pulled aside*
Ooh.

DICKENS:
Mr. Mowchuk, we agreed to a partnership, did we not?

MOWCHUK:
Yes, we did.

DICKENS:
And in a partnership one listens to the suggestions of the partner, does one not?

MOWCHUK:
Yes, that's true.

DICKENS:
Then, as your partner, I suggest we leave.

MOWCHUK:
Maybe she needs our protection.

DICKENS:
Partners act together or not at all.

SADIE:
I didn't think you'd turn your back on a cockfight, Dickens.

HIGHRISE: *seeing the cat*
How's old Puss? What's this? Turned blue since I was here last? Whatsamatter? Caught a chill?

HIGHRISE picks up the cat and strokes it, checking the neck. It's loose.

SADIE:
That was the time of the yellow cat.

DICKENS:
Well, Mowchuk?

HIGHRISE tries to twist the cat's neck off without letting the others notice. His face contorts with the attempt.

HIGHRISE:
Are you going to miaow for me?

SADIE: *taking the cat from him*
You have to work to please Puss.

HIGHRISE:
Her charm.

SADIE:

Good. I like this return to self confidence. While Highrise works you can lick envelopes, Mr. Mowchuk.

She leads him to a stack of correspondence on the dining room table and picks up a colourful advertising pamphlet that unfolds to the floor. She drops it.

That one first, I think.

MOWCHUK:

I'll get it.

MOWCHUK picks up the pamphlet. She smiles. MOWCHUK continues to lick and seal throughout the following.

SADIE: *to DICKENS*

And you can glower. I'll let you know when we're ready for you. *She sits on the footstool beside HIGHRISE.* Now, where have you been and what have you been doing, my tall wicked man? Where have you been? I'll sit as quiet as a little girl in kindergarten.

HIGHRISE: *looking around at the covered furniture*

I'll start here. *Gradually uncovering a delicate chair.* This one comes off gently. I'm undressing a shy young girl. You have to peel her delicate without touching the tender fruit too soon or she'll be frightened. In an absent-minded way, as though it's not important at all, I take her. *He sits on the chair back to front.*

SADIE:

Tell me. Tell me.

HIGHRISE:

More?

SADIE:

And better.

HIGHRISE:

I've an urge to travel. A sea voyage, yes. Fisherman!

SADIE:

I don't like that one.

HIGHRISE:

It only just happened.

SADIE:

Never did like it. The usual, Mr. Highrise.

HIGHRISE: *menacing as he moves behind SADIE*

But I've never told you how a fisherman kills an octupus. He lifts her high out of the water, like this . . . *With a swift movement, he scoops up SADIE's shawl, creating a head with his left fist.* . . . where her tentacles hang ugly and useless. Then, with his shiny sharp teeth he cuts the nerve between her eyes.

HIGHRISE pulls a spring knife from his vest. The blade cuts through the shawl and forward to SADIE's throat. MOWCHUK starts to her defence. DICKENS restrains him.

SADIE:

False teeth.

HIGHRISE raises the weapon high, as if to strike.

It would be your best story and you'd have no one to tell it to with Sadie gone.

Defeated, knowing what she wants, HIGHRISE returns the knife to his vest.

HIGHRISE:

The usual.

Though he's tired, HIGHRISE climbs up on a piece of furniture and assumes the stance of a performer.

MOWCHUK:
What is the usual?

SADIE jumps up and down, laughing and clapping in her excitement. Her applause infuses animation into HIGHRISE, but he waits silently, his eyes on DICKENS and MOWCHUK, who indicate no enthusiasm, though MOWCHUK is curious. SADIE pokes them.

SADIE:
Clap! Come on. Then he'll do it.

They clap. HIGHRISE bows.

DICKENS: *trying to save face by enjoying HIGHRISE's humiliation.* I hadn't hoped for a minstrel show.

HIGHRISE bangs three times with his cane, cutting into DICKENS' line.

The following sequence is played like a vaudeville skit.

HIGHRISE:
I'm working as a car salesman in a clip joint, see. And when I say clip joint, I'm not just beating my gums. The owner not only takes the wool from the sheep, he takes the skin. This guy is so crooked he has to have a special bed made like a pretzel to fit him. So I decide, as I have a strong sense of justice, my downfall, ladies and gentlemen, to get one back at the owner on behalf of all the little folk. I sacrifice myself for them as I do every day of my life.

DICKENS: *sarcastically, to MOWCHUK*
Have you got a hanky?

HIGHRISE:
Besides, he's handed me a few soft cheques.

SADIE: *prompting*
You take a car.

HIGHRISE:
Not just a car. *He pulls a sheet off the tea trolley.*
A Jaguar XKE.

MOWCHUK:
Is that better than a Lincoln?

HIGHRISE: *wheeling the tea trolley around*
So long, suckers! I've taken your debts on me, your dreams, and your hate. Blessed and cleansed be your pocketbooks! They read about me in the papers and, man, they wish me luck like I'm an athlete, every one of 'em wanting to be me but knowing he doesn't have the guts. The lights of the small towns come and go. Come and go.

Appropriate effects from SADIE who switches the overhead lights on and off.

Young girls turn over in their beds and moan as I pass. Then dawn.

SADIE:
Dawn in Wetaskiwin.

HIGHRISE: *shrugging*
Why not? *approaches DICKENS* Excuse me, is this Wetaskiwin?

DICKENS:
What?

SADIE:
Answer him. Go on. Say, "Yes it is, Mister. Looking for anything in particular?" Say it. You're an old cleaning man in the train station.

HIGHRISE:
Torn overalls, yellow moustache, pushing a broom . . .

SADIE:
The smell of banana and orange peel, gum wrappers, half-eaten wieners . . .

DICKENS:
Have you gone mad?

SADIE:
Are you going to play, or would you like to leave?

DICKENS: *grudgingly playing the role*
Are you looking for anyone in particular?

HIGHRISE:
Why yes, my good man . . .

DICKENS bristles.

SADIE:
He can keep his name, can't he, Highrise?

DICKENS:
No one in my family has been in sanitation.

HIGHRISE: *in play*
As a matter of fact, I'm looking for the mayor.

DICKENS:
How would you expect a janitor to know the mayor?

SADIE:
You have that part too.

DICKENS:
A mayor, eh? That's more like it. What was he like? A man of dignity, I'd imagine, with the proper word for . . .

HIGHRISE:
With a paunch and a silver pocket watch and a passingly pretty daughter of about . . . eighteen.

SADIE strikes a simpering pose.

Delightful.

DICKENS: *in role*
May I be of help to you, sir?

HIGHRISE:
I'm looking for a printer to make . . . *He takes out a large colourful lease form.*

SADIE:
Copies of a copy of a leasing form.

DICKENS:
I'd be glad to oblige, but why ask me such a thing?

HIGHRISE:
Well, you see, I, or rather my company, have reason to suspect that the land around your little town, your charming town of . . . er . . .

SADIE:
Wetaskiwin.

HIGHRISE looks around as though to check if anyone is listening.

HIGHRISE:
Mr. Mayor, would you like to become the official most likely to be remembered in the entire history of this region? Instead of being the mayor of Wetaskiwin . . .

SADIE:
. . . the trade centre of the grain belt . . .

HIGHRISE:
How would you like to be the mayor of Wetaskiwin, Oil Centre of the North?

DICKENS:
Oil?

MOWCHUK:
Oil.

SADIE:
Copies of a copy of a . . .

MOWCHUK: *innocently finishing the phrase*
. . . leasing form.

HIGHRISE, from his magical pockets, produces shares and agreements for DICKENS and MOWCHUK to sign.

SADIE:
Go on. Sign.

MOWCHUK:
I don't sign anything I haven't read.

DICKENS:
A man's reputation rests in his name.

MOWCHUK:
This is a contract for a share in a brick company.

SADIE:
Highrise, don't be naughty.

HIGHRISE takes these papers back and exchanges them for other papers.

HIGHRISE: *as though speaking to a group*
I am indeed privileged to be addressing this distinguished assembly of the town council as well as interested fellow citizens, who have kindly gathered here tonight. I assure

you that this honour will be repaid in the same spirit in which it is given.

SADIE:
Hip hip . . .

ALL:
Hooray!

HIGHRISE:
I have with me news that the first drilling begins in two weeks.

SADIE:
Hip hip . . .

HIGHRISE:
Men and machinery are now on their way to Wetaskiwin . . .

ALL:
Hooray!

HIGHRISE:
There will be full employment.

SADIE:
Hip hip . . .

HIGHRISE:
And all for the smallest contribution on your part.

Silence. HIGHRISE sits ceremoniously, hand out, waiting for the money. Neither of the men budge. SADIE goes to the cat, unscrews its head and takes out some money. DICKENS tries to stop her.

DICKENS:
My dear Mrs. Golden . . .

SADIE:
You're obsessed with money today, Dickens.

DICKENS falls back offended, clutching at his collar.

HIGHRISE:
The excitement's been too much for the mayor. His heart.

SADIE pushes DICKENS into his chair.

SADIE: *to DICKENS*
You need a holiday. Yes, you do, daddy.

SADIE AND HIGHRISE: *singing together*
So the mayor decides to go to the . . .

SADIE: *singing alone*
. . . seashore. But before he leaves he says . . .

HIGHRISE: *imitating DICKENS*
"Move into the house, dear boy. Consider yourself a member of the family."

DICKENS: *beaten*
I'll be back in two weeks, when the first of your machinery is due to come in. In the meantime, help yourself to whatever you find in the house.

SADIE:
The mayor's daughter stays behind to be . . .

HIGHRISE:
And since the good man had told me to . . . I . . .

SADIE:
He . . .

HIGHRISE: *with SADIE*
Do.

SADIE: *with HIGHRISE.*
Does.

HIGHRISE has SADIE in his arms, her face turned front. This could be done in tango rhythm, the lines delivered between rhythmic pauses. This business may include singing.

HIGHRISE:
I almost don't bother. I prefer a challenge.

MOWCHUK: *remembering*
The last two . . .

DICKENS: *with disgust*
Civilization.

SADIE crawls awkwardly onto the couch and into a formal sexual position with HIGHRISE over her. Their pose is held briefly, as if for a photograph. A squeak from MOWCHUK marks the moment.

MOWCHUK: *crossing himself*
Our Father which art in . . .

HIGHRISE:
After we empty the fridge and cupboards and drain the last bottles of booze in the house I bid my weeping bride-to-be adieu.

SADIE: *still on the couch*
But she knows he's left her something valuable.

HIGHRISE:
I'd lain with her laughing into her breasts.

SADIE:
She carries his laughter like a foetus. *She sits up and imitates the voice of the mayor, in unison with HIGHRISE.*

SADIE AND
HIGHRISE: *together*
"Help yourself to everything, my boy."

HIGHRISE:
Come on. Move it out.

MOWCHUK and DICKENS act as loaders.

SADIE:
To the van. Waiting outside.

HIGHRISE:
One dining table with teacups, four chairs . . . One tassled couch, very well used, one glass cat . . . one . . . two cases . . .

HIGHRISE picks up DICKENS' and MOWCHUK's cases. DICKENS and MOWCHUK stop loading.

MOWCHUK:
Leave that alone!

SADIE: *annoyed*
You've got no play in you.

HIGHRISE puts the cases on the tea trolley.

Goodbye, my love. Goodbye. *He waves.*

HIGHRISE: *using the tea trolley as a car, moving around the room.* You should see the dust we raise on the highway. Some of the farmers recognize me and wave. Ye blessed little hamlets of tedium, I give thee gossip and hate and cheated fortune to smoke over oil stoves in the harsh white winter. I say unto you, day after day I sacrifice myself without thanks, to bring excitement to the underprivileged.

DICKENS:
I'll expose you and put you in jail. Justice!

HIGHRISE:
I promised you a place in the town's history. Expose me and you expose yourself.

SADIE: *with delight*
Isn't he awful?

MOWCHUK:
What about the town people? All their money?

SADIE:
The good mayor refunded it.

DICKENS:
Out of his own bank account?

HIGHRISE: *at the door*
Regrettable.

HIGHRISE kisses his fingers and waves goodbye as he disappears into the hall, still with DICKENS' and MOWCHUK's briefcases as well as the cat on the tea trolley.

DICKENS:
Hey! Come back. He's got my case.

MOWCHUK:
And mine.

A clatter is heard as HIGHRISE, with the tea trolley, gets stuck in the doorway. SADIE laughs. The two men pursue HIGHRISE to the door.

You, sir, do not exist.

HIGHRISE:
What do you mean I don't?

MOWCHUK:
You went out with the n . . . n . . . nineteenth-century novel. You're an . . . an . . . an . . . anachronism.

MOWCHUK and DICKENS take their briefcases from an unresisting HIGHRISE.

HIGHRISE:
I'm not thirty yet.

SADIE:
You never are. *In the hall doorway, thoughtfully absent* I really ought to tell that story to the police.

HIGHRISE looks worried. SADIE picks up the phone, smiles, then puts it down.

When you get jowly. *She goes into the kitchen.*

DICKENS:
Give me back her money.

HIGHRISE, still considering SADIE's last words, takes the money out of his vest pocket and hands it to DICKENS.

My God, look what she was ready to . . . *DICKENS replaces the money in the cat.*

HIGHRISE:
She would too.

MOWCHUK:
Would what?

HIGHRISE:
Rat on me.

He pushes DICKENS and MOWCHUK out of the way. He collapses into the armchair.

DICKENS:
Hey, that's my chair.

HIGHRISE:
Nothing's yours. It's all hers.

MOWCHUK:

You are tired, aren't you? How old did you say you were?

HIGHRISE:

Shut up. None of them make me work like her. She did call the cops once. Sadie Golden. I spent a night in jail for her, then she withdrew the charge. Said it was a mistake. That's what attracts me. It's talons against talons with us. If we draw blood all the better. Some of them go down like moths in a bottle of formaldehyde, and that's a bore. But the old bitch is taking over. Sometimes when I'm doing things I'm not sure whether it's for me or so I can tell her. Or if I've done them at all. "Where've you been Highrise? Tell me. Tell me." *Aware of MOWCHUK's naive interest.* Say, why don't you buy a share in my brick company. I could see you were taken by the idea.

MOWCHUK:

The logic did fascinate me, the possibility that one could define the ideal environment for every individual.

HIGHRISE:

Yeh. You got it. So why not become a millionaire? Not interested. How about if I name you co-inventor?

MOWCHUK: *taking the bait*

How could you . . .

DICKENS:

Lay off the boy.

HIGHRISE:

I can't help myself. When I see a pigeon with his neck out . . . But you're right. We're brothers.

DICKENS:

No claims to relationship, thank you very much.

HIGHRISE:
La de dah. I'd prefer it weren't so. You two are pathetic examples of our guild.

DICKENS:
She made a fool of you.

HIGHRISE:
And you? But you don't like it. Especially before an audience. If you're not willing to be a jackass, go home, buster. Change professions. We're performers. Artists. If she wanted to see your ass you'd bend over and split your pants to oblige.

DICKENS goes to HIGHRISE. MOWCHUK holds him back.

MOWCHUK:
You crude cr . . . r . . . rook.

HIGHRISE:
Two ends of the same stick. So you're polite, and obviously less stimulating.

DICKENS:
I reject your perforation. We have a grand role. A noble role.

HIGHRISE:
Depends on the customer. Some roll. Some won't.

DICKENS:
I am not being fa . . . fa . . .

MOWCHUK:
Facetious.

HIGHRISE:
Bless you.

MOWCHUK:
You're a fraud. We satisfy legitimate needs.

HIGHRISE:
With books she won't read? Spices she doesn't use?

DICKENS:
We, sir, are the last personal communicants with Sadie Golden.

HIGHRISE:
You think you're a fucking priest. Not so far from me then.

DICKENS:
Ours is a sacrosanct relationship. Not like you.

MOWCHUK:
Not sacred, logical.

HIGHRISE:
She is a Customer.

SADIE is suddenly among them.

SADIE:
You've been talking too much, Highrise. I'll remember that.

DICKENS: *pathetic*
Were they lies?

SADIE:
Everything is true. When I say it. *She deliberately goes to the phone and dials.* Hello? Police Department? *HIGHRISE stiffens.* I've something of interest to tell you. I'm having a party this afternoon. Did you receive the invitations? I know it's against policy, but this one might be . . . *HIGHRISE hangs up the phone.* There was something missing in your performance this afternoon, Highrise. Perhaps your hair is thinning a bit.

DICKENS finds it difficult to conceal his delight. HIGHRISE turns his back to the audience and begins to pull something from his vest.

SADIE: *excited*
Presents?

Feather dusters, one attached to another, emerge as a flowing peacock plume, stiff enough to hold the peacock's crescent shape. When HIGHRISE shakes them, they whirr with the sound of the peacock's feathers in his mating dance.

HIGHRISE:
They're for you. From me. For use. As you will. Red. And gold. And green. And purple. And red. And red. And yellow. And red.

As he speaks, HIGHRISE holds the large duster crown around his shoulders. He takes short strutting steps trapping SADIE in the circle of feathers. She makes quiet frightened anticipatory sounds.

SADIE: *throughout HIGHRISE's dance*
Oh. Oh. Oh. Oh.

HIGHRISE:
I've been high. And low. And in. And out. Theft. Burglary. Fraud. Drugs. Rape. Murder.

SADIE crumples to the floor, legs spread. HIGHRISE scatters the feathers over her in what is obviously a sexual act. This last effort to please SADIE has exhausted HIGHRISE. He slumps on the loveseat. His magical jacket is too heavy for him. He takes it off revealing a surprisingly slight frame.

MOWCHUK:
Holy Mary Mother of God protect me in this hour of need in this house of sin.

DICKENS crawls to SADIE where she lies twitching, then still, under the feathers.

DICKENS:
Mrs. Golden? Are you alright? Are you listening? I've got things to confess. You always said I had no need to. You said I was the only man you knew without a flaw. You said it made you strong and proud just to know me. You said you wondered if I was human.

SADIE: *in a weak voice, from under the feathers*
A weakness for food, you've that.

DICKENS:
But I know now, when you said why should I confess anything to a silly old woman anyway . . .

SADIE sits up, annoyed, blowing away the loose feathers.

I think you didn't mean it . . . And . . . and . . . and now I want to.

MOWCHUK: *horrified*
Mr. Dickens, our agreement. Dignity. Logic. *He trips.*

HIGHRISE:
What's wrong?

MOWCHUK:
Your damn bricks!

HIGHRISE laughs, though exhausted. MOWCHUK tries to move again. He trips again. He's trapped.

MOWCHUK:
I can't move.

DICKENS:
The last year, the bottles I've been bringing you . . . I'm no longer with the company. They've taken to publicity. Television and all that. I'm not needed anymore.

SADIE:
And the bottles? They were filled with . . .

DICKENS:
Coloured water.

Suddenly, a mailbag, even larger than the first one, is thrown through the door.

SADIE:
More mail. You see how they love me. I'm glad you told me, Dickens. And you still insisted on credit. I'll remember that. Now join hands, the three of you. Go ahead. You've given me such pleasure.

They do so. They play ring around the rosie with SADIE in the centre.

It's nearly three o'clock. If only you were babies.

MOWCHUK puts his thumb in his mouth.

I could talk to you then. Babies understand me. And animals.

DICKENS drops on all fours.

HIGHRISE:
Would you like *me* to think of you as my mother?

SADIE:
Yes.

HIGHRISE:
When I'm about to do something very naughty I ask myself, "What would Sadie Golden want me to do? Would she be proud of me or ashamed?"

SADIE:
And what do you do?

HIGHRISE:
What would make you ashamed. Because then you'll be angry. You'll want to spank Highrise. *Bending over a chair for a spanking.*

SADIE:
I've been meaning to have a talk with you.

DICKENS:
I have other things to confess.

MOWCHUK:
You promised. A gentleman's agreement.

DICKENS:
It's my wife. She . . . She makes tea when I want coffee . . . She doesn't pay any attention to me even when I'm being a bad boy.

MOWCHUK:
Mmmmm . . . Mmmmmmmm . . . Mmmmmmmmmm.

The sound of a hurt, angry, wailing child.

SADIE:
Poor little man. Were we ignoring you?

MOWCHUK:
You were. Yes, you were.

SADIE:
Would you like mommy to pat the little tummy? Stretch out on the rug then.

DICKENS:
Me too. Me too.

HIGHRISE is still bent over the chair for his spanking.

HIGHRISE:
Spanking!

SADIE:

I wish I'd known my husband as a baby. Can he see us now, I wonder? You don't know what a temptation helplessness is to a woman. You don't give us credit.

The three men remain in varying positions of childlike vulnerability.

The things we might have done to you and didn't. Holding you in our arms, dependent on our breasts, grasping, pulling at us . . .

The following is as though she were giving a speech.

I have led a full, rich and rewarding life. You think it's just me standing here? I have friends and relatives. While they are alive, wherever they are, so am I. We should be like the tribes in Africa. They all live under one roof. On the mother's side, I read it somewehere. Or no roof at all. That's how it was in the old days. There's no such thing as neighbours anymore. My friends are here. But none of you can suckle from me. It's nearly three o'clock. Before he couldn't have enough of me, Old Man Golden, it wasn't decent, it was cruel, he wouldn't let me alone, when I bled, in the night when I was safe in my dreams he came for me, in the hospital right on the hospital bed, right after I'd had the babies, in the afternoon when even the teacups are sleeping, he'd surprise me, "Now, now," he'd say. Am I real? Do you see me? And then the pain, but "Now," he'd say, "now." These hands, wrinkled, crippled, blue veins, but parchment too, I think. Do you see them? Or through them. *Imitating her husband again.* "You're not here, woman. You don't exist. No, not now. Not tonight." Me not asking, just looking. It changed. Now it's all silence. The smell is musty, yes, but still there is a smell. Is there? "I don't see you," he'd say. "I won't see you." I feel a pain, but is it just a thought? Not even that sometimes, at night, my mind, I think, "Now think," but blank, then white as chalk, not even a colour, not lights even, not . . . *Singing weakly.* A . . . B . . . C . . . Write something. Draw. Like with a pencil. Like with a . . . like . . . you, you see me, touch me.

The men, infants, are incapable of responding.

You're not in the house of a dead woman, are you? Thin, dissolving . . . transparent, like my window. I float into it, yes, I love it, yes, I become this glass and through it, too, dissolve I enter whatever passes in front of my window, a dog or a cat or a man; sometimes I'm the sparks in the wire, or a sound, yes, there are sounds in my street sometimes, the things I've been I'd blush to tell you, through this glass. But when the sun hits it, ohmyGod, the glare, then I'm trapped like a spirit in a white cave crying for a body to enter.

REVEREND CAVIL enters from the kitchen carrying a large briefcase and a Bible.

REV. CAVIL:

Is this the residence of Mrs. Golden? May I come in?

The phone rings. SADIE answers it.

SADIE:

Three o'clock . . . that's right.

WISEMAN enters carrying a case similar to MOWCHUK's, but much larger.

Why, Mr. Wiseman.

Another sack of mail is thrown in through the door. The phone rings. SADIE answers it.

Yes, three o'clock.

All present look at their watches. The front door opens and an enormous sack filled with samples and advertisements is thrown in. It spills on the floor. A salesman enters just behind, walking over the mound. It's the florist, APPLEBAUM, who looks like a rotund wax-figure.

APPLEBAUM:
For you, Madam.

He hands her a large bouquet of wax death flowers. SADIE spreads them over the last sheeted piece of furniture. MILKMAN, LAWYER, DOCTOR – as many representatives of our consumer sales society as the production can afford – enter up the aisles, through the front plate glass window, and, if possible, through the walls. As an alternative, tapes and mannequins may be used.

SADIE scans the salesmen anxiously. A dapper small man dressed in undertaker's costume enters down the staircase from the non-existent second floor. He is wearing white gloves. He hands SADIE a card.

UNDERHILL:
Mr. Underhill at your service.

SADIE:
I've been waiting for you.

The salesmen drop their products to the floor and move in on SADIE, grasping for the cat which she holds out of their reach above her head. Frightened, she lets it fall. It shatters. Money spills from its belly. SADIE goes to the cupboard and opens it, revealing rows of coloured cats. She selects a white cat and returns to the salesmen who are scrambling on the floor for the money.

You're welcome, all of you, welcome in my house.
It can never be said Sadie Golden denied a visitor.
Look, my room is almost completely in flower, and it's you, gentlemen, I have to thank. And now we will have tea.

A serving man enters from the kitchen carrying a huge silver tea tray. He places the tray on the table. SADIE mounts her chair.

But first . . . I will sing for you.

The fly swings in the quivering web.
The fish is pierced in the craw,
It's all for love that you must die
Sang the wise jackdaw.

No. That's not the one. That's not the song.

She opens her mouth. All are polite attention. The sound starts as a moan and builds and builds to a terrible cry, a scream of loneliness and anguish. As the cry builds, the lights rise to an unbearable glare, the three o'clock terror. Even before the cry ends, the salesmen begin to clap politely. The glare is at its peak. Suddenly, rock music blares, continuing SADIE's scream. She falls. The salesmen catch her. UNDERHILL gestures. One of the salesmen pulls the sheet off the last remaining covered piece of furniture – the coffin. The music merges with the howl of a cat. The salesmen place SADIE in the coffin. UNDERHILL closes her eyes and covers her with a sheet. The salesmen raise the coffin and carry it slowly towards the staircase, followed by DICKENS, MOWCHUK and HIGHRISE.

The music dissolves, except for the howl of the cat, now high and thin. The walls move, or, if a scrim, it is pierced by the light. It is apparent now that there is definitely no second storey. The sound ceases abruptly. The cortège moves silently up the stairs to the void.

Blackout.

APPENDIX

The following speeches may be inserted on page 98, replacing the speeches there.

HIGHRISE:

I've an urge to travel. A sea voyage, yes. Fisherman! His boat is moored to a pier. He's smoking and eating sardines out of a tin. "Hey, fisherman, take me to the Queen City." He smiles and wipes his fishy lips on his sleeve. He says nothing. So with this hand, I chop off his head. *Ripping a sheet off a bench which acts as a boat, he sits.* From the water where the pumpkin bobs, I can see the tongue still licking at the corners of the mouth. I use the blood for fuel and the old tank speeds like a jet. The exhaust makes little crying sounds. Glowing fish fly out of the deep and dance around me. But the colours, Sadie Golden, they spread behind me and lap around the sides of my face like a woman's hair. It's better, brighter than the neon signs on Granville Street on Saturday night.

SADIE:

You told me that one before.

HIGHRISE:

I couldn't have. It only just happened.

SADIE:

Two years ago you told it to me. Only better. How old are you, Highrise?

HIGHRISE:

Not yet thirty.

SADIE:

You said that too. *She gazes at him, waiting.* The usual, Mr. Highrise.

TALONBOOKS – PLAYS IN PRINT 1976

Colours in the Dark – James Reaney
The Ecstasy of Rita Joe – George Ryga
Captives of the Faceless Drummer – George Ryga
Crabdance – Beverley Simons
Listen to the Wind – James Reaney
Ashes for Easter & Other Monodramas – David Watmough
Esker Mike & His Wife, Agiluk – Herschel Hardin
Sunrise on Sarah – George Ryga
Walsh – Sharon Pollock
Apple Butter & Other Plays for Children – James Reaney
The Factory Lab Anthology – Connie Brissenden, ed.
The Trial of Jean-Baptiste M. – Robert Gurik
Battering Ram – David Freeman
Hosanna – Michel Tremblay
Les Belles Soeurs – Michel Tremblay
API 2967 – Robert Gurik
You're Gonna Be Alright Jamie Boy – David Freeman
Bethune – Rod Langley
Preparing – Beverley Simons
Forever Yours Marie-Lou – Michel Tremblay
En Pièces Détachées – Michel Tremblay
Lulu Street – Ann Henry
Three Plays by Eric Nicol – Eric Nicol
Fifteen Miles of Broken Glass – Tom Hendry
Bonjour, là, Bonjour – Michel Tremblay
Jacob's Wake – Michael Cook
On the Job – David Fennario
Sqrieux-de-Dieu – Betty Lambert
Some Angry Summer Songs – John Herbert
The Execution – Marie-Claire Blais
Tiln & Other Plays – Michael Cook
Great Wave of Civilization – Herschel Hardin
La Duchesse de Langeais & Other Plays – Michel Tremblay
Have – Julius Hay